Colin Bord was born in London in 1931 and has been a professional photographer for twenty years, working in advertising and public relations as well as freelance, Janet Bord was born in Leicester in 1945 and has worked as a freelance publisher's editor, writer and photographer. The two met through their mutual interest in leys, standing stones and UFOs, and are presently engaged in running a picture library devoted to rural Britain, prehistoric sites and strange phenomena. They are the authors of *Mysterious Britain* (1972), *The Secret Country: An Interpretation of the Folklore of Ancient Sites in the British Isles* (1976), *A Guide to Ancient Sites in Britain* (1978), *Alien Animals* (1980), *Earth Rites* (1982), *The Bigfoot Casebook* (1982) and *Ancient Mysteries of Britain* (1986).

A Guide to Ancient Sites in Britain

selected and photographed by

Janet and Colin Bord

PALADIN
GRAFTON BOOKS
A Division of the Collins Publishing Group

LONDON GLASGOW
TORONTO SYDNEY AUCKLAND

Paladin
Grafton Books
A Division of the Collins Publishing Group
8 Grafton Street, London W1X 3LA

Published by Paladin Books 1979
Reprinted 1979, 1984, 1986, 1988

First published by Latimer New Dimensions Ltd 1978

Copyright © Janet and Colin Bord 1978

ISBN 0-586-08309-X

Printed and bound in Great Britain by
Collins, Glasgow

Set in Monotype Photina

*'Hoary and lichened by age, grim and fretted by a thousand storms,
our ancient megalithic monuments
are still numerous, massive, and full of mystery.'*

Walter Johnson, *Folk-Memory*, 1908

Introduction

Prehistoric Britain

Man's impact on the landscape of Britain is everywhere noticeable, from the sprawling cities and towns of the densely populated areas to the regiments of conifers planted across some of the remoter hills. Indeed the countryside we see today is altogether different from that seen by the earliest inhabitants of Britain, and the changes have been made slowly, over many centuries. Although climatic variations have played some part, the changes were principally wrought by the hand of man, who began by clearing trees and undergrowth with axes and fires so that crops could be grown. Settlements grew up, and very gradually, through Enclosure and Industrial Revolution, the British scene has developed into what we see today.

Considering that the first men are thought to have lived in Britain 500,000 years ago (the Old Stone Age), it is amazing to think that traces of them have been discovered only recently, enough to give archaeologists clues to how they lived and what they ate. There are no *substantial* remains dating back quite so far, but when one considers how many generations have lived and died since the time of the earliest constructions included in this book (around 3500–4000 BC), it is surprising that so many relics of prehistoric Britain have survived.

There is much of prehistoric Britain left for the twentieth-century visitor to explore: 1,000 megalithic tombs, 30,000–40,000 round barrows (in England alone), over 900 stone circles, around 3,000 hillforts and countless thousands of standing stones still survive in varying states of decay or preservation. Only a small number of these could be included in this guidebook, but the sites we have chosen are some of the most interesting. At many of the sites included in guidebooks to prehistoric Britain, there are few visible remains, and such sites are therefore only of interest to the archaeologist. In this guidebook we have taken care to include only sites where there is something to be seen, usually impressive stone structures or banks and ditches, and in our descriptions of them we have given factual information so that visitors will be able to identify what they see.

We have also selected only those sites which are reasonably accessible. Fortunately most of the outstanding sites can be reached easily by car or by bicycle, with, in some cases, a short walk from road to site. To see hillforts to their best advantage often involves uphill walking, so we have not included those hillforts which are particularly inaccessible, and information is given on the length and nature of the walk to those we

have included. If the weather is good, it is well worth the exertion needed to reach the summit of a hill crowned by a fort, because the views are often magnificent, as the photographs sometimes demonstrate. We have tried to make this the first truly pictorial guide to Britain's prehistoric sites, and hope that the pictures will help make this a book which will be enjoyed by the armchair traveller as much as by those who are able to visit the sites.

For those readers who have not studied archaeology, the following brief description of the types of sites included in this book, and the accompanying time chart, will help to put the visible remains into perspective.

Once the last Ice Age had left Britain and the climate became more hospitable, the people of the Mesolithic or Middle Stone Age (10,000 to 4000 BC) probably lived the wandering lives of hunter-gatherers. It was during the Neolithic or New Stone Age (4000 to 2000 BC) that the first lasting structures were erected, the earliest being burial chambers of various kinds. Large slabs of stone were sometimes used in the construction of early tombs, which were then buried under a mound of earth, and many designs of *chambered tombs* have been recorded. Names often used are *gallery grave* (where a stone-built passage leads into the mound, often with side chambers leading off – e.g. West Kennet, Wiltshire) and *passage grave* (where a long, narrow passage leads to the burial chamber – e.g. Maes Howe, Orkney). *Quoit, cromlech* or *dolmen* is usually used to describe a stone tomb whose earth mound has gone, leaving huge upright stones open to the elements, often topped by a large *capstone* (e.g. Pentre Ifan, Dyfed). A *cist* is a small burial pit made of stone, often resembling a stone coffin, within a burial mound (e.g. Kilmartin linear cairn cemetery, Strathclyde Region). Stone tombs were being built before 3000 BC; these and other stone structures are often called *megalithic*, meaning 'of large stones'. From the remains sometimes found inside the burial chambers, it would seem that they were used for the burial of families and/or communities over long periods, the entrance passage being sealed after each burial. Some tombs have been sealed finally, the passage having first been filled with stones. *Barrows* are mounds of earth covering burial chambers, and can be either *long* or *round*. Long barrows date from the Early and Middle Neolithic, while round barrows were usually constructed later, during the Bronze Age (approximately 2100 to 700 BC). In areas where stone was plentiful, the mounds, both long and round, were often built of large pebbles, and are called *cairns*.

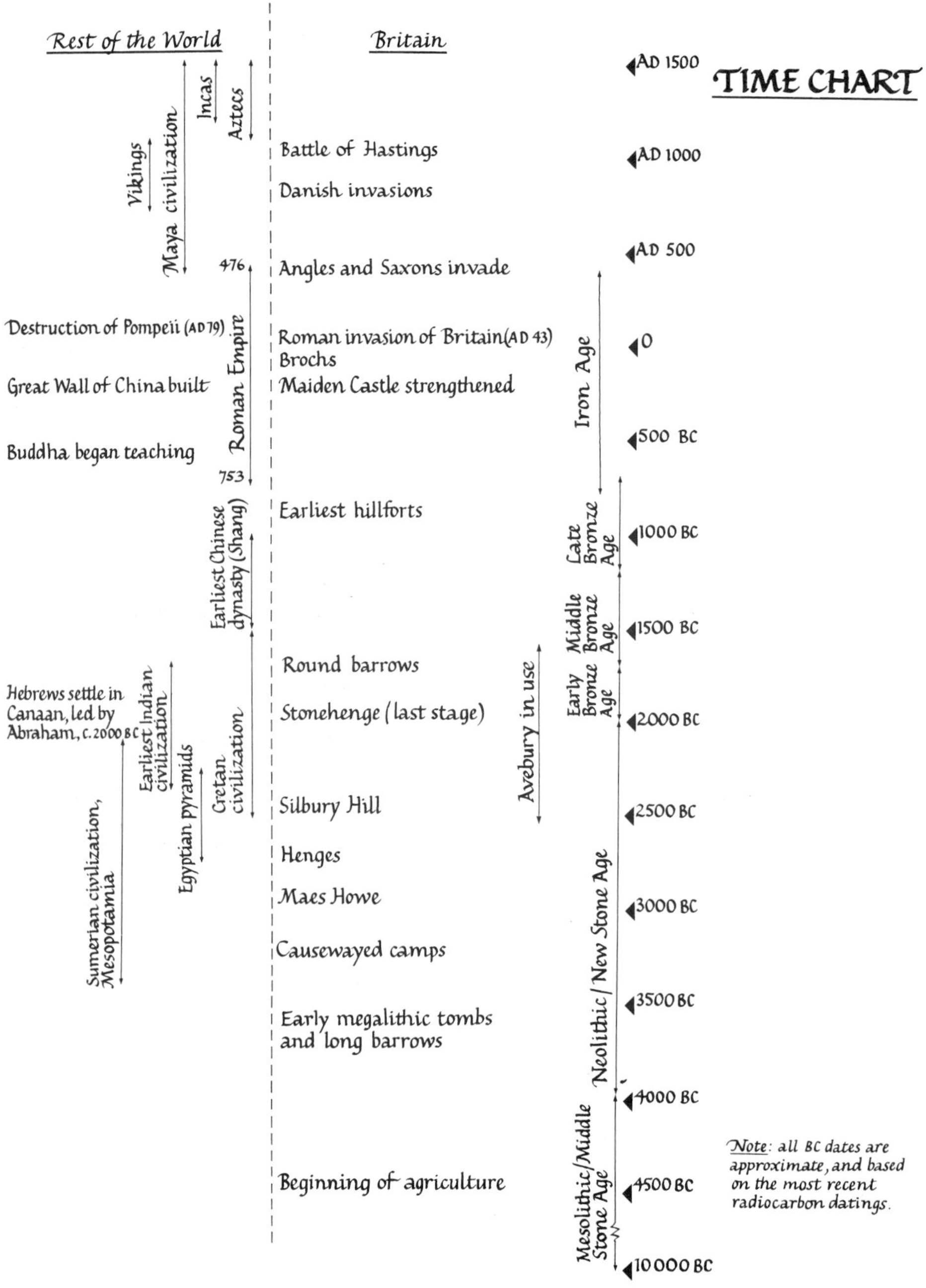

Rest of the World

Britain

TIME CHART

◀AD 1500

Incas
Aztecs
Vikings
Maya civilization

Battle of Hastings   ◀AD 1000

Danish invasions

476   Angles and Saxons invade   ◀AD 500

Destruction of Pompeii (AD 79)   Roman invasion of Britain(AD 43)   ◀0
Brochs

Great Wall of China built   Maiden Castle strengthened

Buddha began teaching

753

Earliest hillforts   ◀500 BC

Roman Empire

Iron Age

◀1000 BC

Round barrows   ◀1500 BC

Hebrews settle in
Canaan, led by
Abraham, c.2000 BC   Stonehenge (last stage)   ◀2000 BC

Earliest Chinese dynasty (Shang)
Earliest Indian civilization
Cretan civilization
Egyptian pyramids
Sumerian civilization, Mesopotamia

Late Bronze Age
Middle Bronze Age
Early Bronze Age
Avebury in use

Silbury Hill   ◀2500 BC

Henges

Maes Howe   ◀3000 BC

Causewayed camps

Early megalithic tombs
and long barrows   ◀3500 BC

◀4000 BC

Neolithic / New Stone Age

Beginning of agriculture   ◀4500 BC

Note: all BC dates are
approximate, and based
on the most recent
radiocarbon datings.

Mesolithic/Middle Stone Age

◀10000 BC

Stones were also used for other building purposes, notably in *stone circles*, most of which probably date from the Bronze Age. They are often described as 'ritual monuments' because until recently there has been no real clue as to their function. Meticulous research by Professor Alexander Thom has shown that circles and *standing stones* (isolated upright stones, often tall and impressive – e.g. Rudston monolith, Humberside) may have been used by prehistoric astronomers studying the movements of sun and moon. The *recumbent stone circles* of Aberdeenshire have a flat stone between two upright stones within the circumference of a circle of standing stones (e.g. Tomnaverie, Grampian Region). *Stone rows* are single or double lines of standing stones running for varying distances across the countryside. Their purpose and date are unknown, though they probably date from the Bronze Age. Many of the best examples are to be seen on Dartmoor, where there are over sixty, but they are usually inaccessible (but see Merrivale, Devon). Another 'ritual monument', found only in the British Isles, is the *henge*, which consists of a large circular area, often containing a stone circle, surrounded by a ditch and bank. Famous examples are Avebury and Stonehenge in Wiltshire, and Arbor Low in Derbyshire, and they usually date from late Neolithic times. Stones of many kinds – *menhirs* (literally 'long stones', i.e. standing stones), those in stone tombs, and also natural outcrops of rock, often lying flush with the ground – display carvings, possibly Bronze Age, called *cup and ring marks*, which comprise a cup in the rock surrounded by concentric circles (e.g. Roughting Linn, Northumberland). Again, the significance of these is unknown, though many theories have been put forward (see page 99, and Evan Hadingham, *Ancient Carvings in Britain*). *Runes* and *ogham* are two types of early writing sometimes found carved on stones (e.g. runes – Maes Howe, Orkney; ogham – The Ring of Brodgar, Orkney).

Causewayed camps are Neolithic hilltop enclosures whose purpose is unclear. They were possibly used as meeting places; their banks and ditches were not strong enough to have been defences. Forts (often called *castles* or *camps*), with a varying number of earth banks and ditches, are a late development, dating usually from the Iron Age (around 800 BC to the time of the Roman invasion), and indicate that fortifications were necessary at that time to help defend people and possessions against local or foreign enemies. *Hillfort* is the most common name used, but there are also *contour forts* where the bank and ditch follows the contour of the hill (e.g. Herefordshire Beacon, Hereford and Worcester); *plateau forts* built on low-lying ground (e.g. Warham Camp, Norfolk); *promontory forts* where defences are built across the neck of a steep-sided peninsula; and *cliff-castles* on rocky coasts, where a headland was defended in the same way as a promontory fort. Traces of *settlements* are often found within hillforts, but these are usually scanty. Far more impressive are the villages (e.g. Chysauster, Cornwall) dating from the late Neolithic to Romano-British times. ('Romano-British' refers to the native British

people at the time of the Roman occupation.) An underground passage or chamber known variously as a *fogou, souterrain* or *earth-house* is sometimes found at or close to such villages (e.g. Carn Euny, Cornwall). Another dwelling structure which has left solid remains is the *broch*, almost unique to the north and west of Scotland, where over 400 are known (e.g. Dun Carloway, Western Isles). These circular drystone towers are thought to have acted as fortified homes during the late Iron Age.

The Romans introduced new styles of architecture to Britain and the numerous remains would require a book of their own, so they have not been included in this guide. However, it is not strictly true to say that we have only included sites dating from pre-Roman times, as there is no precise dividing line. The Iron Age in Britain continued into the first centuries AD, and certain sites, such as the settlements in Cornwall, were occupied while the Romans were in Britain. We have also included one type of site to which the 'pre-Roman' classification does not, or may not, apply, and that is the enigmatic *hill figure* of southern England. Some examples of this art form are almost certainly of very recent date, but others cannot be dated with any certainty, and because of their interest we give the histories of the oldest. (See Cerne Abbas giant, Dorset; The Long Man of Wilmington, East Sussex; Uffington white horse, Oxfordshire; Westbury white horse, Wiltshire.)

Events at the time of the Roman invasions can be dated precisely – for example, Julius Caesar invaded Britain in 55 and 54 BC, and Aulus Plautius' major invasion took place in AD 43 – but before that all dating is uncertain, and until recently was based almost on guesswork. Since the first development of radiocarbon dating techniques in 1946, it has become possible to date sites by calculating the radioactivity of the carbon in an organic sample (wood, charcoal, bones, etc.) from any given site, and the results have been surprising, showing that many sites are older than had been thought. As a result, long-held theories about the origins of civilisations were upset. More recent developments have complicated the dating system beyond description, and those who wish to learn more are recommended to read Colin Renfrew's *Before Civilization*.

HOW TO USE THIS BOOK

As the contents page shows, we have divided the area covered by this book (Britain excluding Northern Ireland) into six sections: southern England; central England; northern England; Wales; central and southern Scotland; and northern Scotland. The distribution of sites chosen for this book may appear to be uneven. The reason is that our pre-Roman ancestors usually built their tombs and other structures on higher ground, in areas where there was a good supply of stone, and so certain areas of Britain are sadly lacking in visually impressive archaeological remains. There are, for example, a great many impressive sites in the south-west and practically none in the east of England. As we remarked earlier, we have been selective in our choice of sites, our two main criteria being impressiveness and accessibility, and so anyone wishing for a guidebook giving all the archaeological remains in a specific area, including the less visually interesting ones, should consult the book list.

If you are touring in a certain county and wish to visit its ancient sites, find the county name on the contents page (page 5) and look up the page number given there. All the sites within that county will be described on the following pages, and if any are close together a map will show their relative positions. See also the key maps at the beginning of each section (pages 13, 47, 95, 107, 131, 147). If you wish to look up one particular site, its page number will be given in the index of sites at the end of the book.

The location of each site is described in detail, and Ordnance Survey map references are given. Except for well-known sites such as Stonehenge and Avebury, it is advisable to use Ordnance Survey maps to locate sites because they are often tucked away down narrow side roads and are easy to miss (sometimes even *with* an Ordnance Survey map!). The scale of Ordnance Survey maps is now 2 centimetres to 1 kilometre (approximately $1\frac{1}{4}$ inches to 1 mile) (1:50,000) – it used to be 1 inch to 1 mile (1:63,360), but this scale was superseded by the metric maps in two stages in 1974 and 1976. The map reference we give for each site applies to both the metric and 1-inch maps, and there is on each Ordnance Survey map an explanation of how this 'national grid reference' is arrived at. The figures we give in brackets after each grid reference are first the new (metric) followed by the old (1-inch) Ordnance Survey map numbers. The old number is given for the benefit of those people who already have the older maps (they can no longer be bought).

However, locating sites on Ordnance Survey maps by means of six-figure grid references is not everyone's idea of fun (though if you have never done it, do not get the idea that it is difficult, for it is not). Also, those who are touring a large area may not wish to invest in a large purchase of Ordnance Survey maps. Such people will find the *AA Great Britain Road Atlas* useful. Covering the whole of Britain except Northern Ireland, the maps in this atlas are to the scale 3 miles to 1 inch, and many of the sites described in our book are marked. For ease in locating each site on a map, we give details of the nearest large town and village, plus the number of miles (as the crow flies, not by road) from town to site, and the compass direction. We also give maps showing the route to the site from the nearest main road. The scale of the maps is shown on them; and north is always at the top. By using the *AA Road Atlas* (or similar) and our maps you should be able to locate the sites without too much difficulty. We would like to stress, however, that Ordnance Survey maps are a good investment if you are touring a fairly small area, because they indicate the whereabouts of all manner of interesting rural features such as holy wells, old crosses, old buildings, and other prehistoric monuments, which are not shown on smaller-scale maps.

Many of the sites in this book are in the care of the Department of the Environment or National Trust and can be visited at any time free of charge. Where there are visiting restrictions and entry fees payable, this is stated. At the more important Department of the Environment sites, descriptive booklets or leaflets can often be purchased. However, a number of sites for which leaflets have been prepared do not have custodians. These leaflets can be obtained from H.M.S.O. or the Department of the Environment (see page 177). Some of the sites are on private property, and although access is usually allowed, visitors are warned not to stray from footpaths or trespass on the owner's generosity in any way. Always observe the Country Code, and keep away from crops, always close gates, do not approach farm animals, and keep your dog on a lead.

Visitors should remember that excavation is *not* allowed at sites, except by experts who have obtained permission to conduct a scientific excavation, and 'excavation' means *all* digging, however superficial and harmless it might appear. Likewise chipping pieces off these ancient stones or otherwise defacing them (which includes climbing on them) is an act of vandalism, for which there is no excuse. Less harmful but equally undesirable is noise or unruliness, which includes the playing of radios. Many people who visit ancient sites wish to absorb the peace and quiet of a hallowed spot, and their visit will be spoiled by unreasonable noise and uncouth behaviour.

We hope you will enjoy your journeys into Britain's prehistory.

Janet and Colin Bord
Powys, August 1976

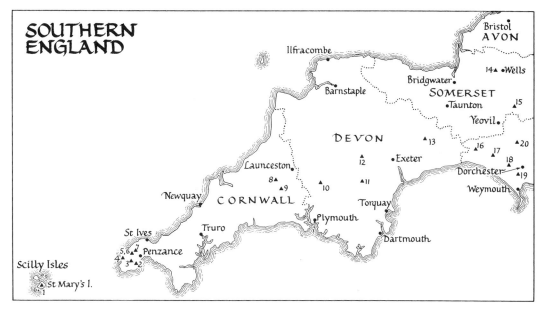

SOUTHERN
ENGLAND

Bristol
AVON
Ilfracombe
14▲ •Wells
Bridgwater
SOMERSET
Barnstaple
▲15
Taunton
Yeovil
DEVON
▲16 ▲20
▲13
▲17
12 •Exeter 18
Launceston ▲16 Dorchester ▲19
8▲ Weymouth
▲9 ▲10 ▲11
Newquay
CORNWALL
Torquay
St Ives Truro Plymouth
5,6▲▲7
4▲ Penzance Dartmouth
▲3▲2
Scilly Isles
St Mary's I.
1

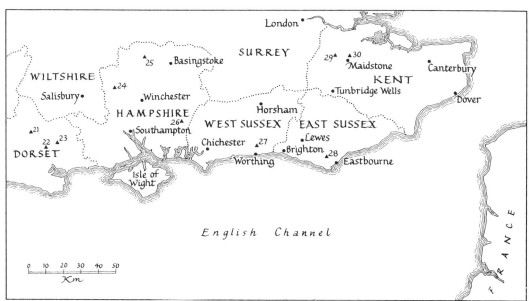

London
SURREY
▲25 •Basingstoke 29▲ ▲30 Canterbury
WILTSHIRE Maidstone
▲24 KENT
Salisbury• •Winchester •Tunbridge Wells •Dover
HAMPSHIRE Horsham
26▲ WEST SUSSEX EAST SUSSEX
▲21 Southampton •Chichester ▲27 •Lewes
22▲ ▲23 Worthing •Brighton 28▲ •Eastbourne
DORSET
Isle of
Wight
English   Channel

F
R
A
N
C
E

0 10 20 30 40 50
Km

1

**Bant's Carn chambered tomb,
Innisidgen chambered tomb
and Porth Hellick Down chambered tomb,
St Mary's, Isles of Scilly**

Of the fifty or so identifiable chambered tombs still to be seen in the Scillies, those we describe here are the best preserved, and all are on St Mary's.

Bant's Carn is in the north of the island, near the northern end of the golf course and on the steepest crest of Halangy Down. It can be reached by footpath from north or south. It is a round cairn

Above *Innisidgen chambered tomb.*
Far left *Bant's Carn before the fallen capstone was replaced.*
Left *Porth Hellick Down chambered tomb.*

Map references:
Bant's Carn
SV 910124 (metric map 203, 1-inch map 189)
Innisidgen
SV 922126 (metric map 203, 1-inch map 189)
Porth Hellick Down
SV 929108 (metric map 203, 1-inch map 189)

about 40 feet (12 metres) in diameter, and the actual burial chamber is 5 feet (1.5 metres) high by 5 feet wide. Four great stones form its roof: one was dislodged during a reputed attempt to destroy the monument in about 1910, and was only replaced in 1970. Piles of cremated bones were found in the chamber, and pottery in the passage leading to it.

Innisidgen chambered tomb is also in the north of St Mary's, and is reached by footpath from the south. The mound is 26 feet (8 metres) in diameter, with a stone chamber 15 feet (4.5 metres) long roofed by five large blocks. Not far away (to the north) is Lower Innisidgen chambered tomb, which is partly covered by sand.

There is a group of five tombs on **Porth Hellick Down** in the south-east of the island (reached by footpath from the north), and one in the care of the Department of the Environment is possibly the best preserved tomb in the Scillies. The mound is 40 feet (12 metres) in diameter, and a curving passage 14 feet (4.3 metres) long leads to a chamber 10 feet (3 metres) long, roofed by four large slabs.

All the tombs have been roughly dated to the Neolithic or Bronze Ages on the evidence of pottery found in them; and all are in the care of the Department of the Environment. The visitor will find the Department's handbook *Ancient Monuments of the Isles of Scilly* very useful.

The Merry Maidens stone circle

Tregiffian burial chamber.
The cup-marked stone is hidden, but
its edge can be seen on the right.

2

The Merry Maidens stone circle,
the Pipers standing stones,
and Tregiffian burial chamber, Cornwall

The Merry Maidens is Cornwall's most perfect stone circle, formed of nineteen stones, each about 4 feet (1.2 metres) high. Though dated to the Bronze Age, little is known about its history or the reason for its construction, but a well-known tradition tells how nineteen maidens were turned to stone for dancing on a Sunday to the music of two pipers, who were also petrified for their transgression of the Sabbath. **The Pipers** are tall stones, 15 feet (4.5 metres) and 13½ feet (4 metres) high, and can be seen in a field not far away to the north.

A little further down the road from the Merry Maidens is a burial chamber called **Tregiffian**, which is worth visiting, especially to see the large cup-marked stone. When the tomb was excavated in 1967, cremated bones and an urn were found.

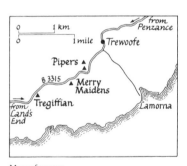

Map references:
Merry Maidens
sw 433245 (metric map 203, 1-inch map 189)
Pipers
sw 435248 (metric map 203, 1-inch map 189)
Tregiffian
sw 430244 (metric map 203, 1-inch map 189)
Nearest town: Penzance
Nearest village: Trewoofe
Location: 4 miles (6.5 kilometres) south-west of Penzance, the stone circle is in a field beside the B3315 road. The stones can be seen from the road, as can the Pipers; the Merry Maidens can be examined, but the Pipers are on farmland. Tregiffian is on the grass verge of the B3315, a short distance to the south-west of the Merry Maidens.

Map reference:
SW 402288 (metric map 203, 1-inch map 189)
Nearest town: Penzance
Nearest village: Sancreed
Location: 4 miles (6.5 kilometres) west-south-west of Penzance, Carn Euny is approached along the twisty, narrow lanes north of the A30 road. Just south of Sancreed a lane leads south-west to the hamlet of Brane, and here there is a car park a few minutes' walk from the site, which is in the care of the Department of the Environment and is open during their 'standard hours'. An admission fee is payable, and a leaflet is available.

An overall view of the settlement

3

Carn Euny settlement and fogou, Cornwall

This Iron Age settlement or village was first discovered by tin miners early in the last century, and there have been several excavations and clearances since then, so that today the site is well laid out and open to visitors. The excavations have

Inside the fogou, looking towards the entrance

shown that there was activity at Carn Euny as early as the Neolithic period, but the first timber huts were built around 200 BC. By the first century BC these had been replaced by stone huts, the remains of which can be seen today. Hearths, post-holes and drains with stone covers can also be identified, and a deep pit lined with china clay and used for storing grain was discovered in 1965. The people who lived at Carn Euny were farmers, stock-breeders, and possibly dealers in tin, and the site was occupied well into Roman times.

The most impressive structure at Carn Euny is undoubtedly the fogou, which is built of stone and extends about 65 feet (20 metres) underground. Fogous (called souterrains or earth-houses in Scotland) have been found at various places in Britain and Ireland, but their purpose still remains a mystery. Suggestions put forward include cattle shed, cold food store, hiding place, and a room for the practice of religious or spiritual rituals. The Carn Euny fogou is a particularly well preserved example, and the circular stone chamber at one end of it is thought to be unique.

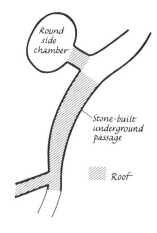

Round side chamber

Stone-built underground passage

Roof

4

Carn Gluze barrow, Cornwall

Carn Gluze (or Gloose; also known as Ballowal barrow) is a complicated structure. Excavation has shown that a pit 7 feet (2.1 metres) deep was first of all dug into the rocky ground. Rough steps led down into it, and it has been interpreted as 'a symbolic entry to the underworld' (Aileen Fox), as no burials have been found there. Four small stone cists stood round the top, containing small pots which possibly held food offerings. A large stone cairn 30 feet (9 metres) by 37 feet (11 metres) was built over all; this would have had a double outer wall and domed roof, but now it only survives to a height of 12 feet (3.6 metres). Stone burial cists were placed just outside this structure, one of which can still be seen. Around the whole tomb a larger cairn or wall 5 feet (1.5 metres) high was built, and an entrance grave containing burnt human bones and Bronze Age pottery was inserted into the outer cairn at the south-west.

This prosaic description of the archaeology of the site gives little indication of the ceremonies or rituals which may have been performed there over hundreds of years, but local tradition has retained a feeling of awe for this ancient burial place. At night-time, miners on their way home from work have seen lights there, and fairies dancing.

Map reference:
SW 355312 (metric map 203, 1-inch map 189)
Nearest town: Penzance
Nearest village: St Just
Location: St Just is 7½ miles (12 kilometres) west of Penzance, and in the village a lane leads westwards to Cape Cornwall and the sea. On the edge of the village, another lane branches off to the left, and this leads within a mile to Carn Gluze, which is immediately to the left of the lane, opposite a tall mine chimney on the right. Carn Gluze is in the care of the Department of the Environment.

5

Lanyon Quoit, Mulfra Quoit, Chun Quoit and Chun Castle hillfort, Cornwall

The south-westerly tip of Britain, known as West Penwith, houses several quoits, of which the three most impressive and accessible are illustrated here. A quoit (also called 'cromlech' or 'dolmen') consists of several tall upright stones surmounted by a large capstone, and archaeologists see these structures as Neolithic burial chambers whose outer covering of earth has dispersed over the centuries. However, it has been argued in opposition to this that small earth barrows have

remained intact, so why should much larger mounds not have survived?

Lanyon Quoit is the best-known Cornish quoit, as it stands right beside the road. It collapsed during a storm in 1815 and was re-erected nine years later, but the reconstruction was not accurate because one of the uprights broke during the collapse and only three were reused. As a result, the quoit is now not so high as it was.

The capstone of **Mulfra Quoit**, up on the moors, has fallen, and the huge stone now leans at an angle against its supports.

Chun Quoit is also on open moorland, and the uphill walk is well worth while because this is perhaps the most visually satisfying of all the

Map references:
Chun Quoit
SW 402339 (metric map 203, 1-inch map 189)
Chun Castle
SW 405339 (metric map 203, 1-inch map 189)
Lanyon Quoit
SW 430337 (metric map 203, 1-inch map 189)
Nearest town: Penzance
Nearest village: Madron
Location: **Lanyon Quoit** stands beside the minor road between Morvah and Madron, about halfway between the two villages and 3 miles (5 kilometres) north-west of Penzance. Nearer Morvah, a lane leads off to the south-west, ending at a farm. Here you can park and **Chun Quoit** and **Castle** are a short walk (approximately 800 yards/720 metres) uphill. Lanyon Quoit is in the care of the National Trust.

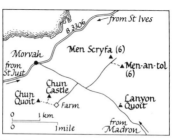

Map reference:
Mulfra Quoit
SW 452353 (metric map 203, 1-inch map 189)
Nearest town: Penzance
Nearest village: Madron
Location: This quoit is rather more difficult to find than the others (see sketch map on page 22). It stands on Mulfra Hill (3 miles/5 kilometres north-north-west of Penzance), but is not visible from the nearest road, a minor road running north-west to south-east between Treen and Penzance. If you are travelling towards Penzance, you should park beside the road about $\frac{1}{4}$ mile (.4 kilometres) after passing a left turn, and walk uphill in a southerly direction for about 500 yards (450 metres). The quoit should then be visible.

Lanyon Quoit has also been called the Giant's Table and the Giant's Quoit.

Mulfra Quoit

quoits. Not far away to the east is **Chun Castle**, a small Iron Age hillfort with tumbled stone walls up to 9 feet (2.7 metres) high in places. Stone gateposts still flank the entrance, and inside are the remains of huts built when the fort was reused in the Dark Ages. There is also a choked well on the north-west side. In 1925 several small smelting pits were discovered here and one contained a piece of slag which proved to be tin. This suggests that the Cornish tin industry has been in existence for at least 2,000 years.

Chun Quoit

The gateway to Chun Castle

6

The Men-an-Tol and Men Scryfa inscribed stone, Cornwall

An old plan of the **Men-an-Tol** (the name means 'stone of the hole') shows that originally the three stones stood in a triangle, but little more is known about this site. It is surmised that the stones are the remains of a Neolithic tomb, because holed stones have been found acting as entrances into burial chambers, but this identification is by no means certain. The Men-an-Tol is best known for the traditional belief that the stones had great healing powers. Naked children were passed three times through the hole and then drawn along the grass three times in an easterly direction. This was thought to cure scrofula (a form of tuberculosis) and rickets. Adults seeking relief from rheumatism, spine troubles or ague were advised to crawl through the hole nine times against the sun. The holed stone also had prophetic qualities and, according to nineteenth-century folklorist Robert Hunt, 'If two brass pins are carefully laid across each other on the top edge of the stone, any question put to the rock will be answered by the pins acquiring, through some unknown agency, a peculiar motion.'

Not far from the Men-an-Tol is the **Men Scryfa** or Screfys ('written stone'), which is an early Christian inscribed stone and strictly speaking is of too late a date to qualify for inclusion in this book. However, it is so close to the Men-an-Tol that a visit to one can easily be followed by a visit to the other. It is a standing stone bearing the worn Latin inscription RIALOBRANI CVNOVALI FILI, which means (the monument of) Rialobran, son of Cunoval, and is probably of late fifth or sixth century date.

Men Scryfa

Map references:
Men-an-Tol
SW 426349 (metric map 203, 1-inch map 189)
Men Scryfa
SW 427353 (metric map 203, 1-inch map 189)
Nearest town: Penzance
Nearest village: Madron
Location: Both sites lie to the north of a minor road between Morvah and Madron, and about 4 miles (6.5 kilometres) north-west of Penzance. Almost opposite the lane leading south-west to Chun Quoit and Castle, a track leads north-east to the two sites. Park at the junction, and walk just over ½ mile (1 kilometre) along the lane. The Men-an-Tol can be seen on moorland a short distance to the right of the lane, after you have passed some farm buildings on the left. Men Scryfa is about 400 yards (360 metres) further along the lane, on the left-hand side. (See sketch map on page 19.)

The Men-an-Tol used to be known as the Devil's Eye.

7

Chysauster settlement, Cornwall

Chysauster is the best-known prehistoric village in Cornwall, where there still remains a well-preserved collection of stone houses 'as old and strange as ruined Pompeii' (Arthur Mee). Compactly arranged, the nine 'courtyard houses', of which five have been excavated, contain features which show how our ancestors lived during the 400 years between 100 BC and the third century AD. The houses are very small (about 88 feet/27 metres long) and all have a passage up to 22 feet (6.7 metres) long into an open courtyard 25–30 feet (8–9 metres) across. Tiny rooms lead off

the courtyard, and the main room, probably the living room, contains a flat stone in the ground with a socket hole which presumably held the wooden post supporting a thatched roof. Also to be seen are open hearths, stone basins for grinding grain, and covered drains. The houses all had terraced gardens. There is a fogou at Chysauster, but it is some distance away from the houses in a southerly direction, and is in a ruined state. It is altogether far less impressive than the Carn Euny fogou (see page 17).

This site was overgrown and neglected for nearly 1,600 years until the first excavations in the 1860s, but in the early nineteenth century people came here to listen to Methodist preachers who liked to use the village as an open-air pulpit.

Map reference:
SW 472350 (metric map 203, 1-inch map 189)
Nearest town: Penzance
Nearest village: Zennor
Location: Chysauster, approximately 3 miles (5 kilometres) north of Penzance, is reached from a lane off the B3311 road north-east of Penzance. There is a car park beside the road, and the site is 500 yards (450 metres) away along an uphill footpath with stiles. It is in the care of the Department of the Environment and is open during standard hours; an admission fee is payable, and a leaflet is available.

Paving at the entrance to Hut 4

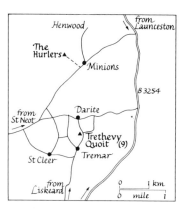

Map reference:
SX 258713 (metric map 201, 1-inch map 186)
Nearest town: Liskeard
Nearest village: Minions
Location: The Hurlers are 4 miles (6.5 kilometres) north of Liskeard, and are on the moor behind Minions. A track leads to them from the minor road which runs through the village. It is not far to walk from the car park beside the road to the circles, which are in the care of the Department of the Environment.

8

The Hurlers stone circles, Cornwall

Out on the wild plain of Bodmin Moor can be found an unusual site – three stone circles close together. They lie in a line but are not the same size. The smallest and most southerly is 105 feet (32 metres) across, the largest is the central circle 135 feet (41.1 metres) across, while the northern circle is 110 feet (33.5 metres) across. Nine, seventeen and thirteen stones respectively survive; they were carefully erected so that they all appear the same height.

The name 'The Hurlers' refers to an old tradition that the circles are men turned to stone. As William Camden wrote in 1587: 'The neighbouring inhabitants terme them *Hurlers*, as

being by devout and godly error perswaded that they had been men sometime transformed into stones, for profaning the Lord's Day with hurling the ball.'

At several sites in Britain it was said to be difficult to count the number of stones, and Dr Yonge in 1675 explained how the problem was overcome in the case of the Hurlers. He said that they are 'now easily numbered but the people have a story that they never could till a man took many penny Loafes and laying one on each hurler did compute by the rem[d] what number they were.' He was lucky; usually something went wrong when this method was tried. For example, at Lower Kit's Coty (30) in Kent the Devil appeared and removed some of the loaves so that the man trying to count the stones got rather confused!

9

Trethevy Quoit, Cornwall

Trethevy Quoit is the most impressive example of
this type of site in Cornwall. It towers 15 feet (4.6
metres) above the ground, and the capstone is 12
feet (3.7 metres) long, with a hole in it. As with the
other quoits described earlier, it is thought that this
may have been a burial chamber covered by an
earth mound, traces of which were said still to exist
in the last century.

Map reference:
SX 259688 (metric map 201, 1-inch map 186)
Nearest town: Liskeard
Nearest village: St Cleer
Location: 3 miles (5 kilometres) north of
Liskeard, the quoit is in a field behind some
cottages and close to a lane between the
hamlets of Darite and Tremar, just under ½
mile (.8 kilometres) from each. It is by a road
junction, and on the left if you are travelling
from Tremar. (See sketch map on page 23.)
The quoit is in the care of the Department of
the Environment.

10

Merrivale stone rows,
stone circle and standing stone, Devon

As a glance at the Ordnance Survey map will
show, Dartmoor is littered with the relics of
prehistory. However, to visit most of them
necessitates a long walk across rough terrain, and
Dartmoor can be a dangerous place to get lost. So
despite the wealth of sites on the moor, we have
included only two in this book, and both are within
sight of the road.

  Stone rows are an enigma: no one is sure why
they were built. They are most common on
Dartmoor, where sixty are known, but the most
impressive examples are also the most inaccessible.
At Merrivale there are three rows, two double and
one single. The double rows run east to west, and
the first one to be reached from the road (200–300
yards/180–270 metres south of the road) is 200

*Trethevy Quoit. The chunk missing from the bottom right of the large flat stone blocking the
entrance may have been cut out in order to provide a way into the burial chamber.*

yards (180 metres) long. It contains around 160
stones, but some are very small. 30 yards (27
metres) further south is a longer row (288
yards/264 metres) containing over 200 stones.
Halfway along it are traces of a round barrow 12
feet (3.6 metres) in diameter, marked by a circle of
stones. The third row is very short, only 47 yards
(43 metres) and with very few stones, leading in a
south-westerly direction.

To the south of the rows, and about 400 yards
(360 metres) south of the road, is a stone circle 62
feet (19 metres) in diameter. It is not very
impressive for the eleven remaining stones are
small, but not far away is a notable standing stone
10½ feet (3.2 metres) tall. All the remains here are
dated roughly to the Bronze Age.

Despite the closeness of the main road, and the
visible signs of civilisation – the quarry at

On the skyline can be seen the low stones which form the circle.

One of the stone rows

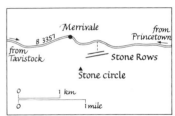

Map reference:
sx 554748 (metric map 191, 1-inch maps 175
& 187)
Nearest town: Tavistock
Nearest village: Princetown
Location: Just south of the B3357 road, 4 miles
(6.5 kilometres) east of Tavistock. The hamlet
of Merrivale boasts a few cottages, an inn,
and an eyesore in the shape of a quarry, and
the stones are on the moorland just east of the
hamlet. There is a place to pull off the main
road about 500 yards (450 metres) past the
inn in Merrivale.

Merrivale and the television station on North
Hessary Tor – among these old stones one seems to
be miles from anywhere, surrounded only by
rough pasture, sheep, and rocky outcrops. There is
in fact so much exposed rock here that it is
impossible to try and pick out the other prehistoric
relics – hut circles and cairns – which have been
identified at Merrivale by archaeologists.

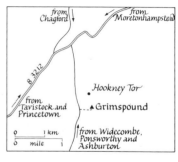

Left *Grimspound as seen from Hookney Tor. The outer wall is clearly defined; the circular heaps of stones within it are the remains of huts. The entrance illustrated in the other photograph is on the far side, at the bottom of the path leading up the hillside.*
Below *Looking through the entrance, across hut circles to the outer wall.*

11

Grimspound settlement, Devon

Grimspound was a late Bronze Age settlement of cattle farmers, and the outer wall encloses an area of 4 acres (1.6 hectares). Within this area are the remains of over twenty huts and several cattle pens. The dwelling huts are to the centre and south, traces of the cattle pens are close to the west wall, and in the north are overgrown store huts. Circles of stones 9–15 feet (2.4–4.6 metres) in diameter mark the hut sites, and stone door jambs and hearths have been identified. Few actual finds were made during the excavation in 1894.

The outer wall has been reconstructed and now stands 10 feet (3.1 metres) wide and around 4 feet (1.3 metres) high. The original entrance gap is in

the south-east wall; all the others (including the one nearest the road) were made later.

A short uphill walk in a north-westerly direction will bring you to the top of Hookney Tor, and from the path there is a good view back over Grimspound as well as down the valley to the edge of Dartmoor.

Map reference:
SX 700809 (metric map 191, 1-inch map 175)
Nearest town: Ashburton
Nearest village: Widecombe in the Moor
Location: 7½ miles (12 kilometres) north-west of Ashburton, Grimspound lies 200 yards (180 metres) to the east of an unfenced minor road across the moor which in the north joins the B3212 Princetown to Moretonhampstead road, and in the south divides and subdivides into a labyrinth of lanes around Widecombe in the Moor. So it is easier to find if approached from the north. The site is about 1¼ miles (2 kilometres) from the main road, and there is room to pull off the lane.

12

The Spinsters' Rock, Devon

This strangely named cromlech was traditionally said to have been erected one morning before breakfast by three spinsters or spinning women, to amuse themselves as they were on their way to deliver the wool they had spun. It fell early in 1862, but with the aid of camera lucida sketches which had been made in 1858, the stones were re-erected in November 1862. (A camera lucida is not a camera in today's sense of the word, but a four-sided reflecting prism by means of which artists and draughtsmen were able to draw the outlines of objects in the correct perspective.)

As with other structures of this kind, the Spinsters' Rock is thought to be the remains of a Neolithic burial chamber, once covered by an earth mound. The tallest stone is 9 feet (2.7 metres) high, and the capstone weighs about 16 tons (16 tonnes).

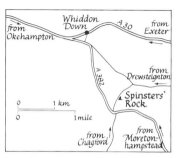

Map reference:
SX 700908 (metric map 191, 1-inch map 175)
Nearest town: Okehampton
Nearest village: Drewsteignton
Location: 7½ miles (12 kilometres) south-east of Okehampton, the Spinsters' Rock stands in a field close by a lane 2½ miles (4 kilometres) to the west of Drewsteignton, and can easily be seen from the lane. However if you wish to examine it more closely, please ask permission from the farm opposite.

13

Hembury hillfort, Devon

Around the beginning of the fourth millennium BC, the southern tip of the spur which later became a hillfort was occupied by Neolithic peoples. Settlements of this type are called causewayed camps, and this particular camp was excavated in 1930–35. Beneath the later Iron Age deposits, a layer of domestic debris was found, together with stone hearths and shallow pits. Food had been stored in the pits, and remains of grain, hazel nuts and pottery were found. Meat and fish may have been cooked in other pits, placed among hot stones and ashes. The grains found could be identified as types of wheat and barley; and this, plus the discovery of querns for grinding the grain, shows that the occupants were arable farmers. Six hundred flint scrapers were also found, and these were probably used to prepare the skins of the animals which they bred.

In the Iron Age, after the settlement had long been abandoned, a fort was built on the hill. Covering $7\frac{1}{2}$ acres (3 hectares), it is triangular in shape, and is outlined by banks and ditches, three on the north and west, two on the east. The entrances were on the west and north-east. This fort was probably occupied in the second and first centuries BC. Later, two banks were built across the centre of the fort, but their purpose is unknown. The site was finally abandoned in AD 65–70.

This restored fine red ware bowl with lug handle comes from the causewayed camp.

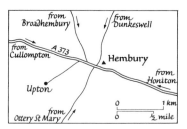

Map reference:
ST 112031 (metric maps 192 & 193, 1-inch map 176)
Nearest town: Honiton
Nearest village: Broadhembury
Location: The fort is to the north of the A373 road, $3\frac{1}{2}$ miles (5 kilometres) north-west of Honiton. There is a layby on the crest of the main road, and from there a short, steep path leads up into the southern part of the fort and to a viewpoint from where on a clear day you can see as far as Dartmoor. The ramparts are best seen at the northern end, and you can either walk there across the fort, or, an easier approach when the fort is deep in bracken, you can drive along a lane which runs along the west side of the fort, and walk up through the woods.

Map references:
Wookey Hole
ST 532480 (metric maps 182 & 183, 1-inch maps 165 & 166)
Hyaena Den
ST 533478 (metric maps 182 & 183, 1-inch maps 165 & 166)
Nearest town: Wells
Nearest village: Wookey Hole
Location: The village of Wookey Hole is only 2 miles (3 kilometres) north-west of Wells, and in the village the caves are signposted. They are privately owned, and open to the public during daylight hours (from 9 a.m. in summer, 10 a.m. in winter). There is a car park; also snack bar, restaurant, museum, and gift shop.

Other caves of archaeological interest in the south-west of England which can be visited are:
Kent's Cavern, Torquay, Devon In Ilsham Road off Babbacombe Road. Occupied during Palaeolithic times; finds can be seen in the Museum of the Torquay Natural History Society in Babbacombe Road. *Map reference:* SX 934641 (metric map 202, 1-inch map 188)
Aveline's Hole, Burrington, Avon Beside the B3134 road in Burrington Combe. Occupied in Palaeolithic times. *Map reference:* ST 476587 (metric map 182, 1-inch map 165)
Gough's Cave, Cheddar, Somerset In Cheddar Gorge beside the B3135 road. A small museum by the cave shows finds from its Palaeolithic occupation. *Map reference:* ST 466539 (metric map 182, 1-inch map 165)

14

Wookey Hole caves, Somerset

In several parts of Britain there are caves which are known to have been occupied at various periods during the 500,000 years BC. Some of these caves can be visited, and there are several in south-west England. Illustrated here is Wookey Hole, now floodlit so that its stalactites and the lake can be seen to their best advantage. It would have been a dangerous place in the days before electricity, and in fact only the first chamber, lit by daylight, was occupied. Pottery found there dates this occupation to the late Iron Age and into the time after the Roman conquest. The discovery of the bones of two goats, a pot, and the remains of a tethering post indicate that part of the outer chamber had also been used as a goat pen; and nearby was found a human skeleton with a dagger, knife, billhook and a stalagmite ball.

It is a long way back in time from this relatively recent occupation of Wookey Hole to the occupation of the Hyaena Den. This small cave nearby was occupied during the Old Stone Age, 500,000 years ago. Excavations in 1852 brought to light the bones of many Ice Age animals – cave lions and bears, mammoths, bison, hyaenas, woolly rhinoceroses, elks and others – as well as flint implements.

15

South Cadbury Castle, Somerset

This large hillfort, 500 feet (150 metres) above sea level and covering 18 acres (7.2 hectares), with extensive views across the surrounding countryside, has impressively sheer sides and is defended by four, and in places five, steep ramparts. The first occupation of the hilltop seems to have been in Neolithic times, and it was not until around 500 BC that the defences of ditches and earth and stone ramparts were started. The fort was occupied at the time of the Roman invasion in

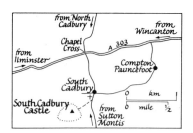

Map reference:
ST 627250 (metric map 183, 1-inch map 166)
Nearest town: Wincanton
Nearest village: South Cadbury
Location: 5 miles (8 kilometres) west of Wincanton on the A303 road, turn south at Chapel Cross and follow the road to South Cadbury. Just beyond the church in the village there is a narrow track leading off to the right. Park here, and continue on foot along the track, which will bring you after a short walk to the north-east entrance of the fort. In wet weather this track becomes a quagmire, and stout shoes or wellingtons are a necessity.

Above *Inside the fort. According to tradition, when the full moon shines King Arthur and his knights, mounted on horses with silver horseshoes, ride round South Cadbury Castle.*
Left *An outer bank and ditch.*

AD 43. It is thought that this was one of the positions taken by Vespasian, the Roman commander who later became emperor in Rome. The remains of thirty people, men, women and children, were excavated at one of the entrances, probably victims of the Roman attack. Some time later, about AD 70, the Roman army broke down the defensive walls and the site became largely derelict for several hundred years.

The association of South Cadbury with 'the once and future king' Arthur is an old one, and goes back at least to the sixteenth century when the antiquarian John Leland wrote: 'at the very south ende of the chirche of South-Cadbyri standith Camallate, sumtyme a famouse toun or castelle'; and: 'The people can tell nothing ther but that they have hard say that Arture much resortid to Camalat'. Nearby are the villages of West Camel and Queen Camel (suggested as the site of the Battle of Camlann), and in the valley to the west runs the River Cam – so perhaps this hillfort is indeed the site of the fabled Camelot.

In 1966 there was a large-scale excavation on the site which has provided information enabling the more recent history of Cadbury to be reconstructed. The site was refortified about AD 470, which is about the time when King Arthur is supposed to have lived, and at this time a wooden hall was built measuring 63 by 34 feet (19 by 10 metres). The scope of this refortification and the building of such a 'feasting' hut indicate that it was carried out by an important and powerful leader, and so perhaps the legends of the great King Arthur are more than fables handed down from the past.

Tradition says that the hill is hollow, and Arthur sleeps within surrounded by his knights, awaiting the time when England again will need their services. Every seventh year, on Midsummer Eve, the side of the hill opens and the ageless king leads his knights out to water their horses at a spring by the church in nearby Sutton Montis. It is also said that when bells were put into the church at South Cadbury, the fairies who lived in the hill left, because spirits do not care for loud noises nor the ringing of bells.

16

Pilsdon Pen hillfort, Dorset

The views from this hillfort, as from many others in this part of the country, are truly breathtaking on a clear day, and the uphill climb is well worth the effort. When you can manage to tear your attention away from the distant scene to your immediate surroundings, you will find that the 8-acre (3 hectares) hilltop is fortified by double ramparts and ditches with entrances on the north and south-west sides. Recent excavation of this Iron Age fort has revealed hut sites, one of which contained a crucible with traces of gold inside it, indicating that this particular hut may have been a goldsmith's workshop. Traces of a large building were found in the centre of the fort, and the head of a Roman ballista bolt was also discovered. A number of mounds within the fort are probably tumuli.

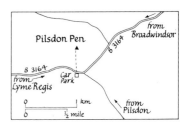

Map reference:
ST 412013 (metric map 193, 1-inch map 177)
Nearest town: Crewkerne
Nearest village: Broadwindsor
Location: The southern end of the hillfort is close to the B3164 road 2 miles (3 kilometres) south-west of Broadwindsor and 5 miles (8 kilometres) south-west of Crewkerne, and the fort is most easily approached from this side. There is a car park by the main road, at its junction with a minor road to Pilsdon. Across the road from the car park a gate leads into gorse-covered moorland (beautiful when in flower) at the foot of the hill, and a clearly defined but steep path points the way up into the fort.

17

Eggardon hillfort, Dorset

'As old as Eggardon hill' is an old west Dorset saying used to describe anything very old. Here three

ramparts and ditches enclose an area of around 20 acres (8 hectares) to form another scenic Dorset hillfort of Iron Age date. Entrances to the south-east and north-west lead into the interior, where a large number of depressions in the ground have been shown by excavation to be storage pits.

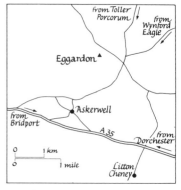

Map reference:
SY 540946 (metric map 194, 1-inch maps 177 & 178)
Nearest town: Bridport
Nearest village: Askerswell
Location: 2 miles (3 kilometres) north-north-east of Askerswell, the hillfort is situated at a crossroads of minor roads, that on the west being a lane which runs alongside the hillfort, on a level with the ramparts. There is a quantity of barbed wire between lane and fort, and so the visitor who wishes to see the interior should park at the widest part of the lane and endeavour to keep to the footpaths, as shown on the Ordnance Survey map.

18

Nine Stones stone circle, Dorset

Even though it is unfortunately situated beside the main road, this small circle of stones retains an air

of mystery as it shelters among the entwining roots and beneath the overhanging branches of the surrounding trees. The tallest block is 6½ feet (2 metres) high, and the others are irregular in shape and somewhat smaller in size, forming a circle about 28 feet (8.4 metres) across.

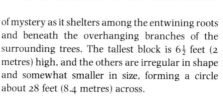

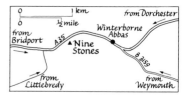

Map reference:
SY 611904 (metric map 194, 1-inch map 178)
Nearest town: Dorchester
Nearest village: Winterborne Abbas
Location: 4 miles (6.5 kilometres) west of Dorchester and just to the west of Winterborne Abbas, the circle is on the south side of the A35 road, within a railed enclosure. There is no parking place on this not particularly wide main road, and it is advisable to visit this site at off-peak hours, when there is less traffic roaring past. The circle is in the care of the Department of the Environment.

19

Maiden Castle, Dorset

This magnificent hillfort, with its great banks standing high above the Dorset countryside, is one of the largest and most impressive sites in England. A thorough exploration of this huge area is a country walk in itself, as the ramparts enclose an area of 45 acres (18 hectares), and it is $1\frac{1}{2}$ miles (2.5 kilometres) around the inner circumference. Much excavation was carried out

It is difficult to imagine the scenes of bloodshed and tumult which have taken place here in the past,
when we now visit this lovely corner of England and see sheep peacefully grazing on the sunlit sloping banks.

Left *An aerial view of the entrance, showing the complex arrangement of banks and ditches possibly designed to confuse invaders. The white 'grains of rice' are sheep.*
Below *An iron arrowhead embedded in the spine of a victim of the Roman attack.*

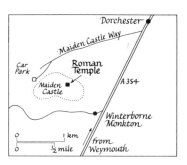

here in 1934–7 and so more is known of the history of Maiden Castle than is the case with many other hillforts. The earliest construction took place about 3000 BC when two lines of ditches were dug to make a causewayed camp at the eastern end of the present site. The shaping of the banks and ditches as we see them today did not take place until much later, between 300 BC and AD 70, and it is thought that the site was deserted for a long period between the original construction and the later enlargement.

The rubbish-filled ditches of the first occupation have revealed flint axes and knives along with tools of bone and horn, and the pieces of pottery also found suggest that the people living there came originally from Brittany. These people deserted their hilltop village about 2000 BC and some time afterwards a huge bank of earth about one-third of a mile (.5 kilometres) in length was constructed, running north-west to south-east down the length of the present enclosure. This strange feature has provided a puzzle for the archaeologists, though it is barely discernible to the visitor today. At the eastern end of this long mound, which may have been a bank barrow, have been found remains which suggest a macabre ritual murder. A man about thirty years old and 5 feet 4 inches (1.6 metres) in height had been hacked to death and completely dismembered before being carefully buried in the mound. By the use of modern radiocarbon dating methods, this murder has now been dated to about AD 635, that is in Saxon times.

During the early years of the present era Maiden Castle contained a flourishing town, but in AD 43 the second Augustan Legion commanded by Vespasian attacked the eastern gateway and, overcoming some fierce resistance, succeeded in subjugating the population. The war cemetery resulting from this encounter has been uncovered just outside the eastern gateway, and in Dorchester Museum can be seen the spine of one of the defenders with a Roman iron arrowhead embedded in the bones. By AD 70 the survivors of the massacre had moved down into the new Roman town of Durnovaria, now Dorchester, and once more Maiden Castle was deserted.

One final development in the hillfort was the building of a small Romano-Celtic temple 40 feet (12 metres) square, in the late fourth century AD. Its foundations can still be seen in the north-east sector of the fort.

Map reference:
SY 670885 (metric map 194, 1-inch map 178)
Nearest town: Dorchester
Nearest village: Winterborne Monkton
Location: On the west of the A354 road just south of Dorchester is Maiden Castle Way. A drive of 1½ miles (2.5 kilometres) along the Way will bring you to a car park, and from there it is an invigorating walk up into the fort. Maiden Castle is in the care of the Department of the Environment, who have a bookstall open during the summer months. A comprehensive guidebook is available, written by Sir Mortimer Wheeler who excavated the site in 1934–7. Objects found in the fort are in the Dorset County Museum in Dorchester.

20

Cerne Abbas giant, Dorset

Here is a giant of untold antiquity cut into the hillside turf. Like the Long Man of Wilmington (page 44), but unlike the Westbury white horse (page 68) and other horses of Wiltshire, this figure is in outline only. He is formed by a trench, 1 foot (.3 metre) wide and the same depth, cut into the underlying chalk, and he is 180 feet (55 metres) high. In his right hand he holds above his head a huge knobbed club 120 feet (36.5 metres) long.

A remarkable feature of this figure is the erect phallus and testicles which undoubtedly indicate that fertility rites were practised here, possibly even before the giant was cut. This is supported by the fact that until recent years, on 1 May maypole dancing and other celebrations were held in the rectangular earth enclosure known as the Frying Pan situated a little further up the hill, above the giant's left arm. These May Day celebrations, once common throughout Britain, were fertility rites to welcome the coming spring, and the maypole was a phallic symbol.

The giant is generally considered to represent the god Helith or Hercules and is thought to have been cut at the end of the second century AD when the Emperor Commodus (who believed he was a reincarnation of Hercules) revived the worship of this ancient god.

A local legend states that a real giant was killed on the hill and that the people from Cerne Abbas drew round the figure and marked him out on the hillside. Women who wished to conceive would spend the night on the figure, and the belief in its fertilising powers has persisted through the ages, some say even up to the present day. Another story ascribes the figure to the monks from the nearby abbey, who cut it as a joke directed against their abbot. Though this is unlikely, it is strange that they did not try to destroy the giant; it was evidently of great significance to the local population. The figure is kept free from grass by a 'scouring' every seven years, the traditional interval for such events. It is remarkable that for

1,800 years the local people have maintained this figure against all those who, for their various reasons, would have gladly seen it fade into oblivion.

Map reference:
ST 666017 (metric map 194, 1-inch map 178)
Nearest town: Dorchester
Nearest village: Cerne Abbas
Location: Cerne Abbas village is 5½ miles (9 kilometres) north of Dorchester on the A352 road. Turn right off the main road into the village and find a convenient parking place. Walk down Abbey Street past the church, and at the end of this street take a path through the graveyard and past the ruined abbey (which will be on your left). Follow the path across a field, bearing left towards the base of the hill; then there is a steep climb uphill. The giant is on National Trust property. A good view of the whole figure can be had from the main A352 road just north of Cerne Abbas.

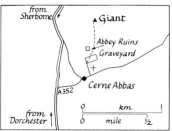

21

Hambledon Hill and Hod Hill hillforts, Dorset

Undoubtedly the most impressive hillfort in Dorset after Maiden Castle, **Hambledon Hill** is encircled by two sinuous ramparts which enclose an area of nearly 24½ acres (10 hectares). It is thought that the present defences were developed over a period of time, but until the site is excavated its history remains conjectural. It was certainly constructed during the Iron Age, however; and there are also the excavated remains of a Neolithic causewayed camp with two banks and ditches to the south-east of the fort. A Neolithic long barrow survived the Iron Age development of the hilltop, and can still be seen, 230 feet (70 metres) long and 6 feet (1.8 metres) high, within the fort about halfway along its length. A walk along the highest rampart round the perimeter of the defences will reveal entrances on the northern, south-western and south-eastern sides. Around 200 hollows within the fort are probably hut platforms.

A short distance to the south of Hambledon Hill is another, smaller, hillfort on **Hod Hill**. This was conquered by the Romans, who built their own fort in the north-west corner. They occupied this during the years AD 43–51.

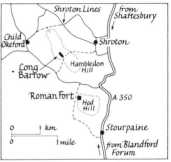

Left *The hillfort on Hambledon Hill. The long barrow can be seen in the narrowest part of the fort.*

Map references:
Hambledon Hill
ST 845126 (metric map 194, 1-inch map 178)
Hod Hill
ST 857108 (metric map 194, 1-inch map 178)
Nearest town: Blandford Forum
Nearest villages: Child Okeford and Shroton
Location: Hambledon Hill lies to the west of the A350 road, around 5 miles (8 kilometres) to the north-west of Blandford Forum, and between the villages of Child Okeford and Shroton. There are several footpaths into the fort: 1. From Shroton Lines (where you can park on the grass verge by the gate into a field); 2. From a lane north-east of Child Okeford, which joins path 1 (see sketch map); 3. From a lane south-east of Child Okeford (with parking in a nearby layby – *not* at the lane end, else you risk having your vehicle towed away by tractor); 4. From Shroton village.
Hod Hill is approached by footpaths: 1. From the A350 road near Stepleton House; 2. From Stourpaine village.

Map reference:
ST 964030 (metric map 195, 1-inch map 179)
Nearest town: Wimborne Minster
Nearest village: Shapwick
Location: Badbury Rings is north of the B3082 road, almost halfway between Wimborne Minster and Blandford Forum (about 4 miles/6.5 kilometres from the former). It is well signposted, and there is plenty of room to park, either close to the road or on the open space nearer to the fort (but the latter necessitates driving along bumpy tracks).

22

Badbury Rings hillfort, Dorset

Three circles of chalk banks and ditches enclose 18 acres (7.3 hectares) of trees at one of southern England's most frequently visited ancient sites. Badbury Rings stands close to a main road, beyond an open space on to which people drive their cars in order to picnic, play ball games, and read their Sunday newspapers, so if you prefer to visit ancient sites in solitude, do not go anywhere near Badbury Rings during a summer weekend (unless you can be there before most people are awake)! Unfortunately the banks are now suffering from the passage of too many feet.

Not much is known about this Iron Age hillfort because it has never been excavated, but seventeenth-century antiquarian John Aubrey mentioned that a 'Roman sword' (probably Iron Age) was found there by villagers, who 'used it as a cheese-toster'. The fort may have Arthurian connexions, for it is one of several places identified as Mount Badon where King Arthur defeated the Saxons in a battle in AD 518. An old tradition told that King Arthur lived on in the form of a raven in the wood which crowns the fort.

Any visitor to Badbury Rings cannot help admiring the superb avenue of beech trees which was planted along the main road 100 years ago by the Kingston Lacy Hall estate. There are said to be 365 of them, one for every day of the year.

23

Knowlton Circles, Dorset

Although only one circle is now clearly visible, there are in fact several circles here. That which has been preserved is known as the Central Circle, and consists of an earth bank, now 12 feet (3.7 metres) high in places, and a ditch 35 feet (10.7 metres) wide. The circle itself has a diameter of 116 yards (106.7 metres) and in its centre are the ruins of a twelfth-century church with a fifteenth-century tower. The Central Circle, and also the others (which will not be described here because they are now only recognisable to a trained eye), is thought to have been a henge monument, a sacred site of Neolithic times.

The presence of a Christian church here indicates the original sanctity of the site. At the time when missionaries brought the Christian faith to Britain there was much opposition, and they found it expedient to take over and reconsecrate the pagans' sacred sites. This was done in order to make the new religion more acceptable to the people, who would then not have to forsake their old places of worship. Consequently there are a number of churches to be found in close proximity to ancient sacred sites, and Knowlton is one of the more impressive examples. The struggle between pagans and Christians over the siting of the churches has also come down to us by way of folklore, and a hundred traditions of this kind can be found in our book *The Secret Country*.

There is also a burial mound 20 feet (6 metres) high at Knowlton, the Great Barrow, and this can be seen clearly from the Central Circle. It is in a field to the east, and is covered with bushes and trees.

Two views of the church and outer bank.

Map reference:
su 024103 (metric map 195, 1-inch map 179)
Nearest town: Wimborne Minster
Nearest village: Gussage All Saints
Location: The Central Circle is beside a minor road just to the north-west of the B3078 road, about 8 miles (13 kilometres) north of Wimborne Minster. There is room to park beside the gate into the site, which is in the care of the Department of the Environment.

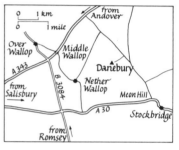

24

Danebury hillfort, Hampshire

This hillfort has recently been carefully excavated, and the findings show that the site has a complex history. The first hillfort was constructed during the Iron Age, in the fifth century BC, but before that, perhaps in the Bronze Age, ritual pits holding tall posts had been placed around the hilltop. Rectangular houses arranged in rows were built about 400 BC, and much work was done to strengthen the gateway and ramparts between 400 and 100 BC. About 100 BC the important east gateway was reconstructed, but whatever the threat at this time, it seems to have proved too strong for the inhabitants of the fort. Within twenty years the new gate had been burnt down and the fort was abandoned. It was in use again for a while at the time of the Roman invasions.

What remains today is still impressive. The entrance-way leads through shallow outer earth-works which were of late construction (after 100 BC) and were used as cattle pens; within is the main rampart surrounding an inner plain of 13 acres (5.3 hectares). All is now covered with beech trees, and the ditch is choked with undergrowth, but in the summer some of the foliage is regularly cut down so that easy access into the fort is ensured.

As would be expected at a site which was occupied for hundreds of years, finds have been many – pottery, currency bars, loom weights, spindle whorls, and human and animal bones. The human bones were widely scattered across the fort as well as being piled in pits, and this evidence, repeated at other sites in Britain, suggests to archaeologists that during the Iron Age the dead were disposed of as simply as possible – by dumping the corpses in pits, or just leaving them lying around to rot. Such behaviour may seem to us unfeeling, when compared with the elaborate burial rituals of the twentieth century, but if, as many people believe, at death the spirit leaves the body, this then is no more than an empty shell which should be absorbed back into the earth from whence it came, as are the leaves of autumn. Perhaps our Iron Age ancestors had ideas more attuned to the natural cycle than we have today.

Map reference:
SU 324377 (metric map 185, 1-inch map 168)
Nearest town: Andover
Nearest village: Nether Wallop
Location: Approximately 4½ miles (7 kilometres) south of Andover, the hillfort lies 1½ miles (2.5 kilometres) to the north-east of Nether Wallop, but cannot be approached directly from that village. A minor road links the A343 with the A30, and the fort lies to the west of this road, about midway between the two main roads. It is signposted, and a lane leads to a car park from which it is a short uphill walk to the fort. This site is one of the Hampshire County Parks.

Map reference:
SU 458572 (metric map 174, 1-inch map 168)
Nearest town: Newbury
Nearest village: Litchfield
Location: 6 miles (9.5 kilometres) south of Newbury and 2 miles (3 kilometres) north of Litchfield, the hillfort is beside the A34 road, and is signposted 'Beacon Hill Picnic Area'. There is a large car park beside the road, from where a path leads straight uphill. Beacon Hill is one of the Hampshire County Parks, and consequently very popular in fine weather.

25

Beacon Hill hillfort, Hampshire

This 12-acre (5 hectares) hillfort high above the surrounding countryside is only reached after a

short and steep but rewarding climb. The ramparts (comprising a bank, ditch and counterscarp bank) are still prominent, and it is possible to walk almost all the way round the fort on top of the bank (almost but not quite, because one corner is fenced off and contains the grave of Lord Carnarvon who discovered Tutankhamun's tomb, and who was at one time the owner of this hill). The bank breaks in the south-east, at the entrance to the fort, and inside are about twenty hut hollows where animal bones and pottery have been found.

The spring-time visitor to this and other hillforts in the south of England should take time off from gazing at the stupendous views to examine the ground underfoot, for many of these sites are rich in wild flowers, blue speedwell and yellow rock rose, cowslip and primrose among them.

Above *Lord Carnarvon's grave is in the top left-hand corner of the fort.*
Left *The ditch and counterscarp bank seen from the main bank or rampart.*

26

Butser Ancient Farm, Hampshire

An extremely interesting research project is currently in progress at Butser Hill near Petersfield, its purpose being to reconstruct and work an Iron Age farm as it would have been around 300 BC. Archaeological investigation has provided information on ancient practices, and this information is supplemented by study of the practices of primitive peoples today, and by material from ancient documents. Many aspects of prehistoric farming are being reproduced – breeding animals, growing crops, building houses, storing food, clearing forests for cultivation, cooking, and making pottery.

Iron Age man had to be self-sufficient. Sheep provided wool to make clothing, also meat and possibly milk. The Soay sheep at the farm come from the St Kilda islands off north-west Scotland, and are the nearest to prehistoric sheep still living today; their bones are very similar to those found in excavations. The cattle used in the Iron Age are now extinct, but those on the experimental farm are of a similar kind, and after training will be used for ploughing and pulling sledges and carts. A variety of crops are being grown, including woad which gives a blue dye, several cereals, beans, vegetables, and flax. Two round-houses have been built with wattle and daub walls and thatched roofs, and another of turf. Prehistoric man kept food in storage pits, and several of these have been dug to find out how long the food could be kept fresh, and whether such pits could have other uses such as water collection. Experiments are also being carried out in pottery making, using different methods of firing the pots.

This brief account hardly does justice to the work being done at the farm, and those who find this aspect of the past particularly interesting are urged to read *Farming in the Iron Age* by Peter J. Reynolds, Director of the Butser Farm Project (see book list, page 178). Visitors are welcome at the farm on special open days, and for more details please write to: The Secretary, Butser Ancient Farm Project, The Red House, Rogate, Petersfield, Hampshire.

Map reference:
SU 717203 (metric map 197, 1-inch map 181)
Nearest town: Petersfield
Location: The farm is on the north of Butser Hill, which is itself 3 miles (5 kilometres) south-west of Petersfield. There is a car park on top of the hill, which is one of Hampshire's County Parks.

This overall view of the Iron Age farm shows: in the foreground, sheep pens with hurdle fences; in the middle distance, two round-houses, and two haystacks on the right, one with a conical thatched roof; beyond the huts, the field system where cereals and other crops are being grown.

Left *The outer rampart, with the South Downs beyond.*
Below *An antler pick and a shovel made from an ox's shoulder-blade, used in flint mining 5,000 years ago.*

27

Cissbury Ring hillfort, West Sussex

The ramparts outlining this hillfort comprised, it has been calculated, 60,000 tons (60,000 tonnes) of chalk, and were protected by a wall of 8,000–12,000 tree trunks at least 15 feet (4.5 metres) long. Although the wood has long since decayed, the ramparts are still impressive, and enclose an area of 65 acres (26 hectares). The outer defences themselves cover 18 acres (7 hectares), and were built in the Iron Age around 350 BC. The bank was 30 feet (9 metres) wide, and outside was a ditch 20 feet (6 metres) wide. The discovery of a spindle-whorl, a weaving comb, pottery, and iron tools shows that the fort was lived in, and its defensive nature is indicated by a find of a hoard of over 400 beach pebbles for use as sling stones. By the time the Romans invaded England, however, the fort had been abandoned.

Around 3,000 years before the Iron Age defences were built, flint mining had taken place on the hill, and traces of the mines can still be seen. About 250 blocked mine shafts have been counted, and they were around 40 feet (12 metres) deep, with galleries leading off. All that can be seen now are hollows overgrown with gorse and bracken, mostly at the west side of the fort. Relics of this Neolithic activity include red deer antler picks (dated by radiocarbon methods to around 3500 BC), shovels made from animals' shoulder blades, and a miner's lamp carved from a lump of chalk. Finds from the fort and mines are in the British Museum and Lewes and Worthing Museums.

A number of folklore traditions relating to the hillfort have survived, including an unusual story about the origin of the hill itself. It was said to have been a lump of earth thrown off the Devil's spade as he dug out the Devil's Dyke north of Brighton. Another tradition tells us that every Midsummer Eve at midnight, Cissbury Ring becomes a dance floor for the fairies. Yet another tale tells of an underground passage leading from the fort to Offington Hall (now demolished) 2 miles (3 kilometres) away. There was said to be treasure at the Cissbury end of the tunnel, but whenever anyone began to dig for it they were frightened away by large hissing snakes which were permanently on guard.

Map reference:
TQ 139080 (metric map 198, 1-inch map 182)
Nearest town: Worthing
Nearest village: Findon
Location: Findon is just north of Worthing, on the A24 road, and a minor road leads east from the village, petering out into a track below the ramparts of the hillfort. There is room to park at this point, and it is but a short climb up into the fort, which is a National Trust property.

28

The Long Man of Wilmington, East Sussex

The Cerne Abbas giant and the Long Man of Wilmington are the only two chalk-cut human figures in Britain, but they are vastly different in appearance. The Long Man is tall (about 230 feet/70 metres), thin and sexless, and holds two staffs or poles. So far- no one has been able to discover when he was first cut, but it is known that the present figure dates from the 1870s when an earlier figure was restored and, it is believed, altered. At this restoration, bricks were used to outline the figure, because previously regular scouring had been needed to keep it clear of turf.

Over the centuries many tales have been told explaining the giant figure's presence, and according to one he was an actual giant who died or was killed on the hill and was outlined where he lay. The 'staffs' held by the figure have given rise to much speculation, and have been variously described as a rake and a scythe, the gates of heaven, Roman standards, spears, and poles surmounted by sun discs. Identifications offered for the figure include St Paul, Mohammed, King Harold, a Roman soldier, Mercury, a Saxon haymaker, Baldur the Beautiful, Apollo, Boötes, Thor, Woden, Beowulf, a surveyor, and an astronomical clock. But so far the strongest clue to the origins of the Long Man is a belt-buckle discovered in 1964 in a seventh-century Saxon grave at Finglesham, Kent. This shows a warrior in a horned helmet carrying a spear in each hand. If a similar figure was carved on the hillslope at Wilmington, alterations made over the centuries, such as by the Puritans and at the nineteenth-century restoration, could account for the differences between the belt-buckle figure and the Long Man as we see him today.

Map reference:
TQ 542034 (metric map 199, 1-inch map 183)
Nearest town: Eastbourne
Nearest village: Wilmington
Location: The Long Man is 3 miles (5 kilometres) north-west of Eastbourne, on the north-facing slope of Windover Hill south of Wilmington, and he is best seen from the minor road leading south from the village. A signposted footpath takes the energetic visitor closer.

29

Coldrum chambered tomb, Kent

The large stones which form the rectangular burial chamber of this Neolithic chambered tomb stand impressively on the edge of a natural terrace, so that when you first see the site the stones seem poised above you on top of a bank. The earth mound behind the burial chamber has almost disappeared, but some of the stones which formed a retaining wall can still be seen on the terrace, though they are now fallen. The photograph shows one of these stones close to, while in the background the burial chamber can be seen.

Excavation revealed the remains of over twenty people, some of whom had suffered from rheumatism. One skeleton found in the burial chamber in the nineteenth century was reburied in Meopham churchyard, causing the vicar of Trottiscliffe to grumble that he had been robbed of his oldest parishioner! Apart from excavational digging, the tomb has suffered from its use in the past as a rubbish tip and chalk-pit, and it partially collapsed when local people dug into it in search of an underground passage said to lead to the church.

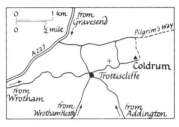

Map reference:
TQ 654607 (metric map 188, 1-inch map 171)
Nearest town: Maidstone
Nearest village: Trottiscliffe
Location: Trottiscliffe village is north of the M20 motorway, 7 miles (11 kilometres) north-west of Maidstone. Trottiscliffe church is to the east of the village, and the minor road passing the church continues in an easterly direction for $\frac{1}{4}$ mile (.5 kilometre) before turning abruptly north. Immediately after this bend is a lane to the right, and a $\frac{1}{2}$-mile (.8 kilometre) walk down this lane brings you to the burial chamber, which is in the care of the National Trust.

30

Kit's Coty House chambered tomb and Little Kit's Coty House, Kent

The diarist Samuel Pepys recorded his impressions of **Kit's Coty House**, already famous in the seventeenth century. He described the remains of the Neolithic chambered tomb as 'three great stones standing upright and a great round one lying on them, of great bigness, although not so big as those on Salisbury Plain. But certainly it is a thing of great antiquity, and I am mightily glad to see it.' The tallest stone is 8 feet (2.4 metres) high, and aerial photographs show traces of a 180 feet (55 metres) long earth mound which once must have covered the burial chamber.

Some people call this site simply Kit's Coty, because 'coty' and 'house' mean the same thing. One story explaining the name says that Kit was Catigern, who fought Horsa in AD 455 and, losing the fight, was buried here. Ghostly re-enactments of the confrontation are said to take place sometimes. Another tradition is that if, at the full moon, you place a personal object on the capstone and then walk round the dolmen three times, the object will disappear, but we cannot vouch for this!

Not far away is **Little (or Lower) Kit's Coty House,** also called the Countless Stones because of a tradition that they could never be counted. This too was a burial chamber, but the stones are now piled on top of one another in complete confusion.

Map references:
Kit's Coty House
TQ 745608 (metric maps 178 & 188, 1-inch maps 171 & 172)
Little Kit's Coty House
TQ 744604 (metric maps 178 & 188, 1-inch maps 171 & 172)
Nearest town: Maidstone
Nearest village: Aylesford
Location: 3 miles (5 kilometres) north of Maidstone, Kit's Coty House stands in a field to the west of, and not far from, the A229 road, though it cannot be seen from the road. A footpath passes it, and it can be approached from either north or south. The distance to be walked from either entrance is approximately ¼ mile (.5 kilometre). Little Kit's Coty House is beside the minor road to Aylesford. Both sites are in the care of the Department of the Environment.

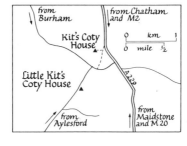

CENTRAL
ENGLAND

Liverpool
Manchester
SOUTH YORKSHIRE
Sheffield
Grimsby

CHESHIRE
Chester
Crewe
Buxton
▲61 ▲59,60
Matlock
Stoke-on-Trent
DERBY-SHIRE
Lincoln
LINCOLNSHIRE
NOTTINGHAM-SHIRE
Nottingham
▲58
Grantham

▲54
Oswestry
Shrewsbury
STAFFORD-SHIRE
Derby
Stafford
▲55
King's Lynn
▲57
Norwich

SALOP
WEST MIDLANDS
Birmingham
Leicester
LEICESTERSHIRE
▲56
Peterborough
NORFOLK

53
▲
Ludlow
HEREFORD & WORCESTER
Worcester
Warwick
WARWICKSHIRE
NORTHAMPTON-SHIRE
Northampton
CAMBRIDGESHIRE
Cambridge
Ely
SUFFOLK

▲52
Hereford
▲51
Banbury
Bedford
BEDFORD-SHIRE
Ipswich

Cheltenham ▲50
▲49
Gloucester
▲32
BUCKINGHAMSHIRE
Luton
ESSEX
Chelmsford

GLOUCESTERSHIRE
46–48
Oxford
OXFORDSHIRE
Aylesbury
HERTFORD-SHIRE
Watford
Epping
▲31

45▲
Swindon
▲33, 34
GREATER LONDON
Reading
Southend

Bristol
Weston-super-Mare
▲44
AVON
43▲
42▲
Bath
36–38▲
▲35
Marlborough
Trowbridge
BERKSHIRE
Reading

▲41
WILTSHIRE
40▲
Salisbury ▲39
HAMPSHIRE
SOMERSET

0 10 20 30 40 50
Km

31

Ambresbury Banks plateau fort, Essex

Beautifully situated in Epping Forest, this Iron Age plateau fort is unfortunately marred by the presence of a very busy main road just a few yards away. 11 acres (4.5 hectares) in extent, the fort is defended by a single bank and ditch, the bank still 4–7 feet (1.2–2.1 metres) high. The original entrance is on the west; that at the south-east is probably medieval. This fort is reputedly the site of Boadicea's battle against Suetonius in AD 61, but there is no reliable evidence for this.

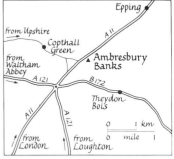

Map reference:
TL 438004 (metric map 167, 1-inch map 161)
Nearest town: Epping
Nearest village: Theydon Bois
Location: Ambresbury Banks is 2 miles (3 kilometres) south-west of Epping, on the east side of the A11 London–Norwich road, almost opposite the minor road to Copthall Green and Upshire. There is room to pull off and park beside the road, though this parking area can become muddy in wet weather.

The ditch below the outer rampart

32

The Rollright Stones, Oxfordshire

The Rollright Stones comprise three separate Bronze Age sites, the most impressive being **The**

though excavations in 1926 indicated that it was natural rather than manmade.

All these stones were once human beings, a king and his army, according to legend. They were marching across the land when they were met by a witch who said to the King:

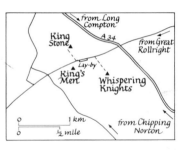

Map reference:
SP 296308 (metric map 151, 1-inch map 145)
Nearest town: Chipping Norton
Nearest village: Long Compton
Location: The stones are ¾ mile (1.2 kilometres) south of Long Compton and 3 miles (5 kilometres) north-west of Chipping Norton, beside a minor road just off the A34 road. The King's Men are by the roadside, the King Stone can be seen in a field across the road, and the Whispering Knights are a short walk down the road and along a footpath by the hedge which borders a field (which is growing a crop or is ploughed, according to the time of year). There is a convenient layby by the roadside very near to the King's Men. The Rollright Stones are popular and much visited, and so anyone who likes to absorb the atmosphere of old sites is advised to visit them very early in the morning. All the Rollright monuments are privately owned, and entry to the circle is by courtesy of the owner, Pauline Flick. A small admission fee is charged.

The King's Men

King's Men, a large circle of about seventy stones looking like huge rotted teeth. The circle is about 100 feet (30 metres) in diameter, and most of the stones are under 4 feet (1.2 metres) high. **The Whispering Knights**, a group of five large stones which once formed a burial chamber, are ½ mile (.8 kilometre) to the east. The name is appropriate, because they do look like a group of leaning men with their heads close together. The four stones which are upright (the capstone has fallen) stand 5–8 feet (1.5–2.5 metres) high. **The King Stone** stands alone behind an iron fence, across the road and in fact in another county, Warwickshire. It is 8 feet (2.5 metres) tall and 5 feet (1.5 metres) wide. A mound which once stood nearby (now reduced by ploughing) was called the Archdruid's Barrow,

Seven long strides shalt thou take,
If Long Compton thou canst see
King of England thou shalt be.

The King's reply was:

Stick, stock, stone,
As King of England I shall be known.

But when he had taken the seven strides, all he could see was the Archdruid's Barrow, which blocked his view of the village in the valley below. The witch cried:

As Long Compton thou canst not see,
King of England thou shalt not be.
Rise up stick, and stand still stone,
For King of England thou shalt be none.

The Whispering Knights

Thou and thy men hoar stones shall be
And myself an eldern tree.

So the King became the solitary King Stone, his men the stone circle, and his knights huddle together in eternal conspiracy.

Although this is the best-known story connected with these stones, there are others of equal interest. One is that the King's Men are uncountable. A baker who tried to ascertain their number by placing a loaf on top of every stone was not successful, because he did not have enough loaves. Various attempts to remove certain stones have ended in disaster.

The King Stone may originally have been somewhat bigger than it is now, because people used to chip pieces off it as good luck charms. They included soldiers who took the chips into battle, and Welsh drovers who came by with their herds of cattle. It is said that dreadful noises were heard when a man, using twenty-four horses, removed the King Stone to his house; so he took it back, only two horses being needed for the return journey. The eighteenth-century antiquarian William Stukeley visited the Rollright Stones, and wrote that near the King Stone was a flat area of turf where, once a year, the young people of the area danced and ate cakes and drank ale. People also used to gather there on Midsummer Eve. They stood in a circle round the King Stone, and when the elder (or 'eldern') tree was cut and bled, the King Stone was said to move his head.

33

**Uffington white horse
and Uffington Castle, Oxfordshire**

Before the gods that made the gods,
Had seen their sunrise pass,
The White Horse of the White Horse Vale,
Was cut out of the grass.

'Ballad of the White Horse', G. K. Chesterton

This strange animal, made on the hillside by cutting away the top turf and revealing the chalky white soil below, is one of the oldest existing figures of this type in the south-west. The only clues to its age are designs found on old coins and on a bucket. These designs show a horse of a similar shape, and the objects bearing them have been dated to the late Iron Age. The horse was at one time thought to have been cut by Hengist, who was an Anglo-Saxon leader in the fifth century AD, and others have suggested that it was cut by King Alfred (who

was born at nearby Wantage) to commemorate his victory over the Danes in AD 871. In fact no one can accurately place the first cutting of this large, enigmatic figure (it is 121 yards/111 metres long) which gallops across the brow of the hillside. As a horse it is not a realistic representation, but is more of an impressionistic rendering with, perhaps, more of a beak than a muzzle, and it has been likened to a dragon. This supposition may find confirmation in the tradition attached to the flat-topped hill in the valley just below, which is called

every seventh year. At scouring time the local people also took part in a 'pastime' in the nearby earth-banked enclosure called Uffington Castle. Various sports and entertainments took place, including foot and horse races, wrestling and cudgelling, and food and drink were provided by the local squire. Another curious feature was that round cheeses were rolled downhill in the combe known as the Manger. In the last century the practices seem to have lapsed, and the horse became very overgrown and was nearly lost.

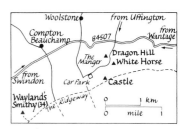

Map references:
Uffington white horse
SU 302866 (metric map 174, 1-inch map 158)
Uffington Castle
SU 299863 (metric map 174, 1-inch map 158)
Nearest town: Swindon
Nearest village: Uffington
Location: On the B4507, 5 miles (8 kilometres) west of Wantage and 11 miles (17 kilometres) east of Swindon, there is a lane leading south, opposite the turning for Uffington village. Follow this lane to the car park, and from there the horse and castle are a walk of approximately ¼ mile (.4 kilometre) across the hilltop. There is a superb view northwards over the Vale of the White Horse, while below can be seen the Manger and Dragon Hill. Because of the flat angle of the hilltop upon which the horse is cut, it cannot be seen as a whole from nearby (unless you are in an aeroplane!), and the best view of it is from the B4508 road 2½ miles (4 kilometres) to the north. The castle, white horse and Dragon Hill are in the care of the Department of the Environment.

The eye of the white horse; in the valley below is Dragon Hill.

Dragon Hill. It was here that St George was said to have killed the dragon, and where its blood spilled there is a bare patch where nothing will grow.

It is remarkable that for 2,000 years this figure has been carefully preserved by the people of the locality. If these chalk figures are not regularly kept clear of grass and plants they can very quickly become obliterated and lost. The cleaning is known as scouring and traditionally took place

Uffington Castle is on the hilltop a short distance away from the horse. It is an enclosure of 8 acres (3.2 hectares), formed by a single bank and ditch and counterscarp bank, with an entrance in the west. Some excavation was done in 1850, when it was found that the ramparts were made by heaping chalk rubble between two rows of posts, and the discovery of an Iron Age coin linked the site with the Dobunni tribe.

Three of the upright stones, seen from the mound behind them. Some of the stones forming the burial chamber are in the foreground.

Map reference:
SU 281854 (metric map 174, 1-inch map 158)
Nearest town: Swindon
Nearest village: Compton Beauchamp
Location: 10 miles (16 kilometres) east of Swindon and 6 miles (9.6 kilometres) west of Wantage, Wayland's Smithy lies about ¾ mile (1.2 kilometres) south of the B4507 road. Take the track opposite the turning to Compton Beauchamp, and follow it until it crosses the Ridgeway, which is the first junction. Leave your vehicle here and walk along the Ridgeway to the right for about ¼ mile (.4 kilometre). Wayland's Smithy is in a clump of beech trees to the right of the track. (See sketch map on page 53.) The Ridgeway is a wonderful place to be on a summer's day, but it can become very muddy in wet weather. Wayland's Smithy is in the care of the Department of the Environment.

34

Wayland's Smithy chambered long barrow, Oxfordshire

If you are visiting the Uffington white horse, it is a pleasant walk on a fine day along the green Ridgeway track to Wayland's Smithy, which is about a mile away within a grove of beeches. The tomb consists of an earth mound 196 feet (60 metres) long and 50 feet (14.6 metres) wide at its widest point. At the entrance to the 20-foot (6 metres) long burial chamber are four erect sarsen stones 10 feet (3 metres) high; originally there were probably six of these. During excavations in 1919, about eight skeletons, one of a child, were found in the tomb. Later excavations in 1962–3 established that the barrow was the second to be built on the site, and the structure visible now was superimposed upon a much smaller mound, both being constructed around 3500 BC.

The name 'Wayland's Smithy' has been attached to this tomb since the tenth century, and the legend which accompanies the name says that if a traveller's horse has lost a shoe, he need only leave the animal there, and a coin on one of the stones. Upon returning later, he will find the money gone and his horse newly shod. This attractive legend has been often repeated, being used by Sir Walter Scott in *Kenilworth*, and in *Tom Brown's Schooldays* whose author, Thomas Hughes, was born in nearby Uffington.

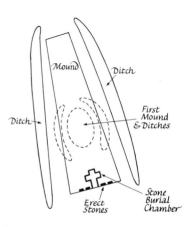

35

Barbury Castle hillfort, Wiltshire

Here on the edge of the Marlborough Downs, where the land drops away to the plain below, is perhaps the most atmospheric of Wiltshire's many impressive hillforts. Enclosing an area of 12 acres (4.7 hectares), two strong ramparts and deep ditches are broken by entrances to east and west. Finds here dating from the Iron Age include chariot fittings and jewellery, and aerial photography has revealed traces of huts and storage pits.

The ancient road the Ridgeway runs along the edge of the downs just below Barbury Castle. In a southerly direction it passes the Hackpen horse (an unimpressive nineteenth-century hill figure), and shortly afterwards reaches its starting (or finishing) point within a mile of the great monument at Avebury. To the north-east of Barbury Castle the Ridgeway crosses at the foot of the downs the lane you will follow to reach the hillfort.

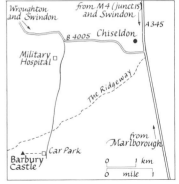

Map reference:
SU 149763 (metric map 173, 1-inch map 157)
Nearest town: Swindon
Nearest village: Wroughton
Location: Only 4 miles (6.5 kilometres) south of the outskirts of Swindon, the hillfort is signposted 'Barbury Castle Country Park' at the road junctions around Chiseldon and Wroughton to the north, and a lane leads directly to the large car park, where there are toilets and pictorial information about other interesting sites in the area. The hillfort is a short walk across the fields; the gate is behind the toilets.

36

Avebury henge, Wiltshire

Although perhaps not so immediately impressive as Stonehenge, Avebury is another henge monument that is justly famous. This unique site covers an area of some 28 acres (11.5 hectares) enclosed by a ditch 30 feet (9 metres) deep and 15 feet (4.5 metres) wide. The outer bank is nearly a mile round and its height was originally 55 feet (17 metres) from ditch bottom to bank top: it is still very impressive. It has been estimated that the construction of this Avebury enclosure would have required some 1,500,000 man hours.

Around the flat central area stand the remnants of a circle of sarsen stones, each stone weighing about 40 tons (40 tonnes) or more. The stones were left rough and not dressed as were the Stonehenge blocks. They were originally obtained from the nearby Marlborough Downs (as were those used at Stonehenge), and there were about 100 of them when the circle was first completed, but today, even after restoration earlier this century, there are only twenty-seven in place. Where the restorers found evidence of a stone hole in the chalk subsoil, the spot has been marked by a small concrete post.

Inside the circle there are other apparently random stones standing. These are the remnants of two smaller stone circles, each containing originally about thirty stones. Many of the missing stones have not been moved far from the circle. In fact they are still in sight, but have been reduced to small lumps and used for building some of the houses of Avebury village. Perhaps if the village, which lies principally within the area of this great circle, had not developed here, there would be far more of the stones still standing now.

There are four entrances in the outer bank, which carry the roads of today, and excavations have shown that three of them are original entrances, and so probably the fourth is too.

In the seventeenth and eighteenth centuries there was much destruction of the stones, and the antiquarian William Stukeley (1687–1765) tells us that 'The barbarous massacre of a stone here with leavers and hammers, sledges and fire, is as terrible a sight as a Spanish Atto de fe [*auto-da-fé*]'. The method of destruction was to dig a pit alongside the stone, line it with straw and wood, then topple the stone into the pit. A fire would be lit, and when the stone was sufficiently hot, cold water was dashed on to it and vigorous blows struck with hammers. This treatment caused the stone to shatter. The stones that remain today are mostly there because they were buried during the fourteenth century, possibly in an attempt by the Christians to eradicate what they considered to be the remains of a pagan temple. The most complete section of the stone circle, in the south-western quadrant (not far from the car park), was extensively cleared

Map reference:
SU 102699 (metric map 173, 1-inch map 157)
Nearest town: Marlborough
Nearest village: Avebury
Location: Some 6 miles (9.5 kilometres) west of Marlborough, the small village of Avebury is bisected by the busy A361 road, and there is a Z-bend in the centre of the village. A lane branches off one of the bends and leads to a car park, where there is also a book stall at peak periods. Nearby are toilets. The quickest way to the stones from the car park is to turn right out of the car park and a few yards further down the lane turn left through a wicket gate. This gives access to the south-west section of the circle, which is the most completely restored part. All the stones are accessible via wicket gates from the road, and it is also possible to make an almost complete circuit of the outer bank, nearly 1 mile (1.5 kilometres) round.

Many of the archaeological finds are in the Avebury Museum, which is further down the lane from the car park, behind the church. Avebury is in the care of the Department of the Environment and the National Trust, and a guidebook is available.

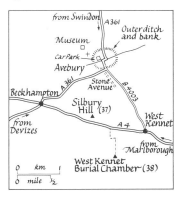

Far left *The aerial view shows the henge in relation to Silbury Hill.*
Left *Three of the stones within the henge.*

and restored during the 1930s, but since then no work has been done on the site and it is possible that there are more stones awaiting excavation in other sectors.

Unlike Stonehenge, there are no known astronomical alignments at Avebury. The central area where the smaller stone circles were is now so built over that it would probably be impossible to find sufficient evidence to establish that Avebury was used for astronomical computations as Stonehenge seems to have been. But as Professor Alexander Thom has shown (in his book *Megalithic Sites in Britain*), many of the stones that were erected elsewhere at this time have significant alignments with the sun's and moon's risings and settings, and it is possible that this is also true of Avebury.

Pieces of pottery found in different parts of the site indicate that Avebury was in use over a period of about 1,000 years from around 2600 BC to 1600 BC. It is supposed by some people that ceremonies were enacted within the central area, perhaps with the 'congregation' or spectators having a good view from the top of the outer bank, but there is no evidence that this did in fact happen, and as with many other sites, its real use remains unknown. Some archaeologists have seen possible significance in the shape of the stones which, generally speaking, seem to be of two basic shapes used alternately: a tall pillar shape and a broad diamond shape. These, they think, could represent male and female, indicating that Avebury was dedicated to the gods of fertility. Avebury has no known connection with the Celtic Druid priests who came much later and practised their rituals within oak groves. It was the romantics of the eighteenth century who linked the Druids with stone circles, as little or nothing was then known about the age of these mysterious structures.

Although such an ancient site might be expected to harbour many traditions and ghost stories, there are in fact very few. On two occasions people have witnessed strange happenings there. During the First World War, Edith Olivier, author of books on Wiltshire, was driving through Avebury at twilight when she heard music and

saw the lights of a fair among the stones. Later she learned that it was at least fifty years since a fair had been held there. Another time, many small figures moving among the stones were seen on a bright moonlit night, and the witness described the feeling as most uncanny.

From the southern entrance of the Avebury circle there runs for 1½ miles (2.5 kilometres) the West Kennet Avenue, comprising 100 pairs of large stones approximately 50 feet (15 metres) apart. The northern third of its length has been restored and can be seen in the fields on the right when leaving Avebury along the road to Marlborough. The stones average 10 feet (3 metres) in height, and they alternate in shape between tall, narrow stones and those of a broad lozenge shape, as in the Avebury circle. Originally the avenue terminated at a small stone circle known as the Sanctuary on top of Overton Hill. This site was lost until excavations took place in 1930, and its layout is now marked with concrete posts. Situated beside the busy A4 road and opposite a popular transport cafe, the Sanctuary completely belies its name and is best avoided by all except the dedicated archaeological researcher.

Above *Destruction of the Avebury stones dramatically illustrated by William Stukeley, who called Avebury 'the most august work at this day upon the globe of the earth'.*
Below *Part of the West Kennet Avenue.*

37

Silbury Hill, Wiltshire

This huge green mound is the largest manmade prehistoric mound in Europe. Although big enough to be a natural hill, it is of such a regular shape that it is obviously the work of skilled hands. The base covers an area of $5\frac{1}{4}$ acres (2.2 hectares) and the hill is 130 feet (39.6 metres) high. The flat top, 100 feet (30.5 metres) across, has in the past been used for playing cricket, though the turf is hardly up to Lords standard. In the eighteenth century local people would meet together on the top every Palm Sunday, when they ate cakes and figs and drank sugared water.

Archaeologists calculate that Silbury Hill took 18 million man-hours to construct, and the vastness of the building project can be more easily comprehended if it is realised that every man,

Map reference:
SU 100685 (metric map 173, 1-inch map 157).
Nearest town: Marlborough
Nearest village: Beckhampton
Location: Silbury Hill is beside the A4 road, 5 miles (8 kilometres) west of Marlborough. (See sketch map on page 57.) There is a layby at the base of the mound. At the time of writing (mid 1976) the monument was closed to allow re-establishment of the turf. If this is the case at the time of your visit, please respect the notice and content yourself with an overall view of the hill, which is in the care of the Department of the Environment.

woman and child in Britain today could together build a mound of about the same size if they contributed one bucketful of earth each. According to the latest calculation using radiocarbon dating methods, Silbury was built around 2500 BC.

At various times the hill has been dug into in an attempt to discover its purpose. In 1776 the Duke of Northumberland brought tin miners from Cornwall to dig a shaft down from the top centre, but nothing could be found. At that time archaeological methods were quite primitive and so some present-day archaeologists fear that valuable evidence went unnoticed and was destroyed. In 1849 a tunnel was dug into the centre from the base and various exploratory side galleries were also dug, but again no trace of a burial was found. The most recent excavation was during 1968–70, when Professor Richard Atkinson had another tunnel cut into the base, partly following the 1849 tunnel. Although he was able to find out much about the methods of construction used, again no trace of a burial was found.

Traditionally King Sil is said to be buried here, sitting on horseback. One version of the legend says he is wearing golden armour, another that he is in a golden coffin, and a third that there is a lifesize figure of gold buried. About the beginning of this century, Moses B. Cotworth advanced the theory that Silbury was 'a gigantic sundial to determine seasons and the true length of the year'. He suggested that a large pole had been erected on top and its shadow used for the calculations. More recently, Michael Dames has identified Silbury as the winter goddess (see his book *The Silbury Treasure*).

The burial mound of an important king or chieftain; the hiding place of a great treasure; a gigantic sundial; the winter goddess. . . We are no nearer now to knowing the real reason for the building of Silbury Hill than were the men of earlier centuries, but, as they did, we still visit and marvel at this impressive pile.

Silbury Hill seen from West Kennet long barrow.

38

West Kennet chambered long barrow, Wiltshire

This impressive Neolithic tomb, situated on a hill overlooking Silbury Hill, is one of the largest and most easily accessible chambered long barrows in Britain. As one approaches, the length of the grass-covered mound can be seen along the crest of the hill ahead. It is more than 320 feet (100 metres) long and 8 feet (2.4 metres) high, and at the left end is a row of large, upright sarsen stones which were used to seal the chamber, and which were repositioned in 1956 after the latest excavations. Behind these is the burial chamber which runs back into the mound about 33 feet (10 metres) and has two small chambers on either side of the central passageway. The roof of the chamber is some 7½ feet (2.3 metres) high.

Before the age of scientific excavation the mound had been damaged by indiscriminate digging, and it is recorded that in 1685 a Dr Toope from Marlborough dug up human bones in order to make 'noble medicine' with which to treat his patients. Later, in 1859, the mound was excavated more carefully, and again in 1955–6. These excavations found a total of forty-six burials ranging from babies to old people. It is thought that this tomb was in use for as long as 1,000 years. At the end of this period the passage and chamber were filled up to the roof with earth and stones, among which were found pieces of pottery, bone tools and beads.

The visitor can walk into the burial chamber and see for himself the massive stones from which it was constructed, but it is rather dark and a torch will be necessary to appreciate fully the skill which went into the building of this tomb over 4,000 years ago. It might be best not to visit the barrow at sunrise on Midsummer Day, because according to tradition, it is visited at that time by a ghostly priest and a large white hound.

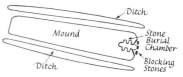

Map reference:
SU 105677 (metric map 173, 1-inch map 157)
Nearest town: Marlborough
Nearest village: Avebury
Location: West Kennet long barrow is south of the main A4 road and is signposted about ¼ mile (.4 kilometre) west of West Kennet hamlet and 1 mile (1.5 kilometres) east of Beckhampton. (See sketch map on page 57.) A small layby provides parking space for two or three cars. The barrow is a walk of ½ mile (.8 kilometre) uphill, and in wet weather and when the field has been ploughed, it can become rather muddy. Keep to the footpath round the edge of the fields, and take a torch if you have one available. This site is in the care of the Department of the Environment who have prepared a leaflet, and objects found during excavations can be seen in the museum at Devizes.

The entrance to the burial chamber is behind the huge blocking stone.

39

Figsbury Ring hillfort, Wiltshire

A ditch and bank enclose 15 acres (6 hectares) at Figsbury Ring, with the bank still 11 feet (3.4 metres) high, and there are original entrances on the west and east: in these respects it is a typical, straight-forward hillfort. However this site holds an archaeological mystery which has not yet been satisfactorily solved, and that concerns the second ditch which was dug inside the fort and can still be seen (it shows up well in the aerial photograph). It varies in width and in depth and so seems unfinished. It is unlikely to have been dug to supply material for the bank because if that were the case it would have been dug much nearer. It may have been an early defensive ditch dug before the hillfort was built, when the site may have been a causewayed camp or henge.

During excavations in 1924, six cooking holes containing charcoal and flints were found, also pottery fragments, and in 1704 a Bronze Age leaf-shaped sword was ploughed up.

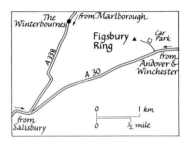

Map reference:
SU 188338 (metric map 184, 1-inch map 167)
Nearest town: Salisbury
Nearest village: The Winterbournes
Location: The fort is only 3 miles (5 kilometres) north-east of Salisbury, and just north of the A30 road. It is signposted, and a very rough lane leads to a sizeable car park, from where it is a short walk to the fort, which is in the care of the National Trust.

40

Stonehenge, Wiltshire

Of all the ancient sites in Britain, this is probably the most impressive, and certainly the best known. Standing in isolation on the wide expanse of Salisbury Plain, it is to many visitors at once a familiar and yet strange sight – familiar because of the thousands of photographs that have been published, and strange because no picture can do justice to the magnificent concept of this huge stone construction. The photograph above shows the famous outline silhouetted by a winter sunset.

The main features of Stonehenge can be seen here: the outer sarsen circle, the inner trilithons, the outer bank and ditch with the Slaughter Stone gleaming in the sun, and the beginning of the Avenue with the Heel Stone in its centre, beside the main road.

The tallest stones are the uprights in the centre group of trilithons (trilithon = two upright stones supporting a third across the top). The tallest of these is 22 feet (6.7 metres) high and has another 8 feet (2.4 metres) below ground. This weighs about 45 tons (45 tonnes). The stones in the outer circle are slightly less massive, but these form the well-known Stonehenge outline of a row of openings. These stones are no rough lumps of material but have been carefully shaped in several ways. First observe the tops of some of the uprights which have lost their lintel, or top, stone. A 'knob' can be seen projecting from the top of the stone, and this is part of the mortice and tenon joint which locked the lintel in place on top. Also the lintels were dovetailed into each other. The lintels of the outer circle were also shaped on both inner and outer faces to make a smooth curve round the circle, and the uprights were also shaped, with a slight bulge in the middle to alter the apparent perspective, perhaps to make them appear even taller to someone standing below and looking up.

Current archaeological research shows that these stones were erected nearly 4,000 years ago. Carvings of a Bronze Age dagger (c. 2100 BC) and axe heads can be discerned on the righthand upright of the trilithon furthest from the present entrance (i.e. the most southerly stone) in a suitable sidelight. Beyond the stone circle is a low earth bank and ditch, and this, along with the Heel Stone which stands alone by the roadside, is even earlier. It has been dated to 4,600 years ago, and is thought to have been the first construction on the site.

This great edifice has suffered over the centuries from the depredations of local people who, ignorant of its value, broke up and dragged away many stones to use for building purposes, and in more recent centuries visitors would stop at Amesbury to hire a hammer, which was used to chip off lumps of stone as souvenirs.

The foregoing is a brief outline of some of the more interesting features of Stonehenge. For greater detail and a fuller understanding of the significance of what you will see, there is an informative guidebook available at the site.

One of the massive trilithons (stone 53 and 54). Beyond is all that remains standing of another trilithon. Note the detail of the tongue on the top of the stone which would have fitted into a corresponding socket on the lintel. Bottom right is a bluestone.

Although popularly connected with the Druids and their supposed sacrifices, Stonehenge was completed long before they came to Britain (which was around 250 BC, nearly 2,000 years after Stonehenge was finished). It was the romantic notions of the eighteenth-century antiquarians which populated the site with Druids and named the Altar Stone and the Slaughter Stone, and it is now thought unlikely that human sacrifice was ever practised here. As with many other ancient sites, its true purpose remains unknown, though recent research has resulted in some startling conclusions. In 1963 a professor of astronomy, G.S. Hawkins, announced that Stonehenge had been built for astronomical purposes, the alignment of stones pinpointing the positions of the midsummer and midwinter sunrises and sunsets, likewise those of the moon. It was also, he said, used to calculate eclipses of the moon. Although not all his ideas are fully accepted by archaeologists, there is little doubt that these features were part of the reason for the construction of Stonehenge. Read his book *Stonehenge Decoded* for the details.

Stonehenge's astronomical possibilities were in fact noticed many years ago, as the following quotation from the *Scotsman*'s Notes and Queries section of 31 July 1875 shows. The writer states that 'a party of Americans went on midsummer morning this year to see the sun rise upon Stonehenge. They found crowds of people assembled . . . The point of observation chosen by the excursion party was the stone table or altar near the head of, and within the circle, directly looking down. The morning was unfavourable, but, fortunately, just as the sun was beginning to appear over the top of the hill, the mist disappeared, and then, for a few moments, the onlookers stood amazed at the spectacle presented to their view. While it lasted, the sun, like an immense ball, appeared actually to rest on the isolated stone of which mention has been made.' Commenting on this, a writer in the *New Quarterly Magazine* for January 1876 said: 'In this we find strong proof that Stonehenge was really a mighty almanack in stone; doubtless also a temple of the sun, erected by a race which has long perished

without intelligible record.' It is true that no intelligible record exists, but both geology and folklore have provided clues to help solve the mysteries associated with the erection of Stonehenge, apart from the evidence unearthed by archaeologists.

Though some of the smaller stones, the bluestones, were probably brought from the Prescelly Hills in south-west Wales, the larger sarsen stones are thought to have come from the Marlborough Downs a few miles away. But ancient legends suggest that all the stones came from Africa by way of Ireland, where they were set up by a race of giants who used their healing properties. Then they were known as the Giant's Dance, and were later moved by the wizard Merlin to the present site, by decree of King Aurelius. He had them erected as a monument to commemorate the treacherous action by Hengist the Saxon who had murdered a British prince and his commanders while they were conducting a peace treaty. In 1724 Daniel Defoe noted in his *Tour Through England and Wales* a local tradition about an unsuccessful attempt to count the stones: 'a baker carry'd a basket of bread, and laid a loaf upon every stone, and yet could never make out the same number twice.'

The stones have now had 'official' numbers allotted to them, so that counting them should be no problem. However, despite the vast amount of research which has been done, there is still controversy about Stonehenge's function, and probably always will be. This noble structure remains an enigma.

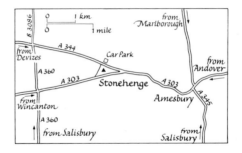

Map reference:
SU 123422 (metric map 184, 1-inch map 167)
Nearest town: Salisbury
Nearest village: Amesbury
Location: Stonehenge is 2 miles (3 kilometres) west of Amesbury on the A344 road and about 10 miles (16 kilometres) north of Salisbury. There is a large car park on the opposite side of the road, from which a subway leads to the stones. This monument is in the care of the Department of the Environment, and is one of the few sites where admission is strictly controlled and an admission fee is charged. Opening hours are: March–April 9.30–17.30; May–September 9.30–19.00; October 9.30–17.30; November–February 9.30–16.00. There is also a book stall, a snack bar, and toilets.

In December 1976 it was announced that the Department of the Environment was considering restricting visitors' access to Stonehenge. The monument receives three-quarters of a million visitors every year, and this has not unnaturally resulted in severe turf erosion. Also some of the stones are being visibly worn away by contact with people's feet and fingers. If the Department does decide to restrict access (at the time of going to press no decision had been announced), visitors will have to view the stones from outside, and will not be allowed to walk among them.

Westbury white horse presents a strange, 'beaked' appearance when seen from the footpath along the edge of the downs (see page 68).

41

Bratton Castle hillfort and Westbury white horse, Wiltshire

There are a number of hill figures cut into the Wiltshire chalk, but the oldest is the **Westbury white horse**. The horse we see today was the work of a Mr Gee, who in 1778 remodelled an existing horse, and in so doing changed it completely. A drawing of the original horse shows a strange creature with a crescent moon on the end of its long, thin tail; the animal also faced in the opposite direction from the present horse. The origins of the first horse are uncertain, though one tradition says it was made in AD 878 to celebrate one of King Alfred's battle victories.

Just above the horse are the ramparts of a hillfort – **Bratton Castle**. The steep banks and ditches enclose an area of 25 acres (10 hectares), and within this area is a long barrow 230 feet (70 metres) long and 12 feet (3.7 metres) high. Several excavations in the barrow have revealed iron objects and urns as well as various burials, though so far only quern stones and a number of large pebbles (possibly sling stones) have been found elsewhere in the hillfort, which probably dates from the Iron Age.

Map reference:
ST 900516 (metric map 184, 1-inch maps 166 & 167)
Nearest town: Trowbridge
Nearest village: Bratton
Location: The sites are on the edge of the downs, between Westbury and Bratton, and 4½ miles (7 kilometres) south-east of Trowbridge. The white horse can be clearly seen on the hillside from the B3098 road which joins the two villages, but the best route up to the top is along the minor road leading south-west from Bratton. This road goes through the hillfort, and there is room to park just beyond. It is only a short walk to the edge of the downs, where, besides being able to look down on to the horse, you will have a marvellous view across the countryside (if you can ignore the monstrous cement works which seems to have been sited to deliberately spoil this view). Both horse and hillfort are in the care of the Department of the Environment.

One of the deep ditches forming Bratton Castle hillfort. The long barrow inside the fort can be seen on the left, just above the top of the bank.

Map reference:
ST 735572 (metric map 172, 1-inch map 166)
Nearest town: Bath
Nearest village: Wellow
Location: 5 miles (8 kilometres) south of Bath, the barrow is on a hill above the Wellow Brook, in very remote and unspoilt country. Drive to Stoney Littleton Farm (the most direct way, to avoid a labyrinth of lanes, is via a minor road from the A366) and call at the farm to collect the key (a small fee is charged). There are signposts along the ½ mile (.8 kilometre) walk. It is advisable to take a torch, and stout footwear if the weather is wet. The barrow is in the care of the Department of the Environment, who have prepared a leaflet.

42

Stoney Littleton chambered long barrow, Avon

Although there is an uphill walk across the fields to reach it, this Neolithic long barrow is well worth the effort needed to get there, for it is one of the finest in Britain. The grassy mound covers a stone-built passage 48 feet (14.6 metres) long, which has three pairs of chambers leading off it. The passage is narrow, and only 4 feet (1.2 metres) high in places, and when you reach the end and turn to look back along the tunnel, the distant patch of light marking the entrance gives a vivid indication of how far you have penetrated into the mound.

The day we visited this site, Britain was in the middle of a heat wave, and after we had slowly climbed the long hill carrying all our heavy photographic equipment, to crawl inside the barrow was a blissful sensation, for it felt as cold as an icebox.

The first excavation was carried out in 1816, and entry was gained through a hole originally made about 1760 by a farmer who took stone for road mending. Human bones, some burned, were found in the burial chambers. In 1858 the barrow was restored, and an inscribed plaque commemorates this work. Not far from this plaque, on the stone forming the south-west door-jamb, can be seen a fine ammonite cast.

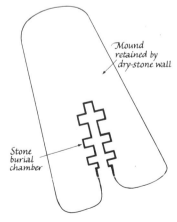

Mound retained by dry-stone wall

Stone burial chamber

43

Stanton Drew stone circles, Avon

This site is considered by some to be nearly as important as Stonehenge or Avebury, and though it does cover a large area it is not visually so impressive as either of those better-known sites. Even so, it is still an interesting place to visit. It consists of three stone circles and a group of stones known as the Cove. The largest circle, called the Great Circle, is about 370 feet (113 metres) in diameter, and twenty-seven of the original thirty stones can be seen, though only three are still standing. Beside the Great Circle is the North-East Circle, about 100 feet (30 metres) in diameter, with eight stones in its circumference, four of which still stand. On the north-east side of each of these circles are some apparently random blocks which are the remnants of two stone avenues (similar to the West Kennet Avenue at Avebury) which appear to have merged into one just beyond the North-East Circle and probably continued towards the lower ground by the River Chew.

All these stones are in a field which is used as pasture for cattle. With so many huge blocks lying about, farm machinery cannot be used, but when antiquarian John Aubrey visited the circles in 1664 the field was growing a crop of barley, which prevented him from accurately mapping the stones. The hand tools of that age enabled the farmer to work among the stones.

The Cove is some distance away, near The Druid's Arms inn, and consists of three stones, two of which are still standing. The third circle is halfway between the Cove and the Great Circle and today has eleven stones, all recumbent. It is on private land and not open to the public.

Although the Cove is beside the village inn which bears the sign of The Druid's Arms, the 'Drew' in the village name derives from a family of that name who were local landowners in the thirteenth century. 'Stanton' is derived from the Anglo-Saxon *stan* (stones) and *tun* (farm or village). The erection of the stones is thought to have taken place in late Neolithic times, which is long before the Druids were in Britain. No excavations have taken place, but Stanton Drew's

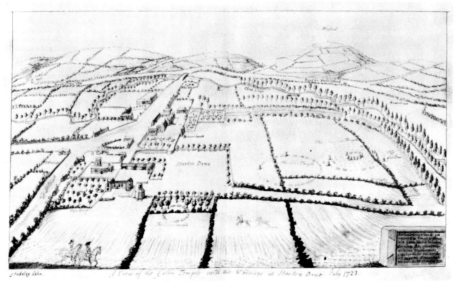

Left *'A View of the Celtic Temple calld the Weddings at Stanton Drue July 1723' by William Stukeley.*
Right *Three of the stones today, with Stanton Drew and the church in the background.*

similarity to such sites as Avebury has enabled archaeologists to date it.

There are several traditions on record, the best known of which tells how a wedding party was turned to stone. As William Stukeley recorded it in 1743: 'This noble monument is vulgarly called the Weddings; and they say, 'tis a company that assisted at a nuptial ceremony thus petrify'd. In an orchard near the church is a cove consisting of three stones . . . this they call the parson, the bride and bridegroom. Other circles are said to be the company dancing: and a separate parcel of stones standing a little from the rest are call'd the fidlers, or the band of musick.' It seems that a wedding party which had been celebrating throughout Saturday night continued into Sunday morning. The fiddler refused to play after midnight, so the dancers were pleased when a stranger clothed in black came on the scene and started to play for them. He played to an ever-increasing tempo, and

the hypnotised dancers were unable to stop. Only when dawn broke did the music stop, and the daylight revealed a terrible scene – the dancers had been turned to stone. The fiddler, who was the Devil in disguise, said he would some day return and play for them again: but they are still awaiting him.

Another tradition, shared with Stonehenge, the Rollright Stones, and other sites, is that it is not possible to accurately count the stones. In 1750 John Wood wrote: 'No one, say the country people about Stantondrue, was ever able to reckon the number of these metamorphosed stones, or to take a draught of them, though several have attempted to do both, and proceeded till they were either struck dead upon the spot, or with such an illness as soon carried them off.' When Wood himself made a count of the stones, a cloudburst followed, and the villagers were sure that the first event was the cause of the second.

Map reference:
ST 601634 (metric map 172, 1-inch map 166)
Nearest town: Bristol
Nearest village: Stanton Drew
Location: Stanton Drew is 6 miles (9.5 kilometres) south of Bristol, and south of the B3130 road. If you are travelling in a southerly direction into the village, the road will curve right in the centre of the village and at this point you should follow the lane on the left. About 50 yards (45 metres) further on, turn left and find your way round one or two corners to Court Farm, where you pay your admission fee for entry to the two stone circles. To view the Cove, return to the road through the village and continue south. Just past The Druid's Arms the Cove can be seen on the left, contained within its own wire fence, and you can walk up to it. There are no specific parking areas, and drivers should find a non-obstructive parking spot in the village. The sites are in the care of the Department of the Environment, and the circles are signposted in the village. A leaflet is available.

44

Worlebury Camp, Avon

A hill which overlooks the sea on the north and the town of Weston-super-Mare on the south was fortified in the Iron Age, and the 10-acre (4 hectares) site still reveals evidence of this early occupation. On the north and west the cliffs acted as a defence, and a single rampart and ditch protected the steep southern edge, but to the east

the local Woodspring Museum, in Weston-super-Mare.

Although it is so near to a typical twentieth-century seaside holiday resort and all that goes with such a place, this hillfort has a strange atmosphere. It is not unpleasant, but almost magical, as if at any minute a gnome might emerge from behind one of the ivy-covered trees. We saw no gnomes on our visit, but we did see a squirrel rustling through the trees, the only sign of life in a wood strangely quiet, with no birds to be heard.

Map reference:
ST 317626 (metric map 182, 1-inch map 165)
Nearest town: Weston-super-Mare
Location: The hillfort should be approached from the northern end of the seafront in Weston. Follow Paragon Road inland, turn right into South Road, and first left into Trinity Road (opposite Holy Trinity church). Trinity Road is a dead end, and there is room to park. From here, steps lead uphill into the fort and a sign 'Encampment' points you in the right direction. Once inside the woods, there are paths in all directions, but a main track leads east to the rubble ramparts (about 500 yards/450 metres). The fort can also be approached from Worlebury, through the woods to the east.

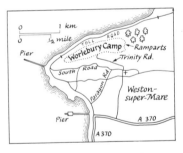

where the ground is level, two stone ramparts and five ditches were constructed. The remains of these are still impressive, the ramparts being more than 10 feet (3 metres) high. Within the hillfort, especially to the east, over ninety storage pits have been discovered, and they are still easy to see, being about 5 feet (1.5 metres) deep. Pottery, iron spearheads, and charred grain have been found inside them. Most of the finds from this site are in

Above *The tumbled stone ramparts.*
Left *This skull showing clear sword cuts, and an iron knife, were both found in Worlebury Camp. The remains of eighteen skeletons have been found there, some of them showing signs of violence, and this, together with other evidence, suggests that at some time the fort was attacked, possibly by the Romans or by Belgic invaders.*

45

Sodbury Camp, Avon

Sodbury Camp, a fine Cotswold hillfort of the Iron Age, is rectangular in shape and covers an area of about 13 acres (5 hectares). The double ramparts on north, east and south are widely spaced, being approximately 100 feet (30 metres) apart; but the outer rampart, which in places is 12 feet (3.7 metres) high, appears to be unfinished.

46

Uleybury hillfort, Gloucestershire

Recognised as the finest hillfort in the Cotswolds, Uleybury is defended by two banks and ditches and has an interior area of 32 acres (13 hectares). There are several breaks in the ramparts, but this Iron Age site has never been excavated and it is therefore not certain which were the original entrances. There are fine views over the valley.

Map reference for Sodbury Camp:
ST 760825 (metric map 172, 1-inch map 156)
Nearest town: Bristol
Nearest village: Little Sodbury
Location: The fort is just outside Little Sodbury, which is 12 miles (19 kilometres) north-east of the centre of Bristol. The shortest approach is from the west, where a lane leads past the manor house just to the south of Little Sodbury. A signpost indicates the Cotswold Way, and this should be followed up into the camp. Where the track divides, sunken lanes run north and south along the outside of the camp. Only a grass verge is available for parking; don't block the entrance to the manor house!

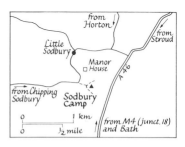

Sodbury Camp

Map reference for Uleybury hillfort:
ST 785988 (metric map 162, 1-inch map 156)
Nearest town: Stroud
Nearest village: Uley
Location: 4½ miles (7 kilometres) south-west of Stroud, the fort is situated on a hill above Uley; on the north-east at Crawley Hill it abuts the B4066 road. There is a small parking area on this hill at the bend, and from there a track leads uphill to the fort.

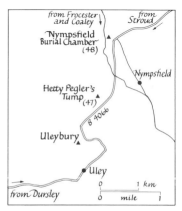

Uleybury hillfort

47

Hetty Pegler's Tump chambered long barrow, Gloucestershire

This grassy mound, named after the wife of a seventeenth-century owner of the field in which it stands, was not recognised as a chambered tomb until 1821 when men digging into it for road-building material broke into one of the burial chambers. As a result of this accident, the north-east chamber was destroyed and is now blocked off; likewise the north-west chamber, which was found to be beyond restoration. The two chambers on the opposite side of the passage are in good repair, however, and can be inspected. There is also a fifth chamber at the end of the passage. The walls are built of large stones, and the passage is 22 feet (6.7 metres) long, 4½ feet (1.4 metres) wide, and 5 feet (1.5 metres) high. Fifteen human skeletons were discovered during the excavations in 1821, plus pottery fragments, charcoal and boars' tusks. A skeleton accompanied by three Roman coins had been placed above the north-east chamber, this being a later burial made long after the tomb was built in Neolithic times.

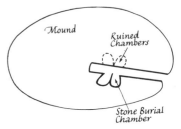

Map reference:
so 789000 (metric map 162, 1-inch map 156)
Nearest town: Stroud
Nearest village: Uley
Location: 1 mile (1.5 kilometres) north of Uley and 3 miles (5 kilometres) south-west of Stroud, the tomb is beside the B4066 road, where it is signposted 'Uley Tumulus'. (See sketch map on page 73.) There is just about room to park on the grass verge, and it is only a short walk across a field to the tomb. It is kept locked, so if you wish to go inside (and you will need a torch for this), you should call at Crawley Hill Farm, Uley (second house on the right on the way to Uley) to collect the key. A small admission charge is payable, and the site is in the care of the Department of the Environment, who have prepared a leaflet.

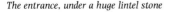

The entrance, under a huge lintel stone

Map reference:
SO 794013 (metric map 162, 1-inch map 156)
Nearest town: Stroud
Nearest village: Nympsfield
Location: The barrow is close beside the B4066 road about 4 miles (6.5 kilometres) south-west of Stroud, and you should look out for the sign 'Coaley Peak Picnic Site'. Pull off here (there is plenty of room to park), and the barrow is at the southern end of the picnic area, beside the trees. (See sketch map on page 73.)

48

Nympsfield chambered long barrow, Gloucestershire

Although the stone-built chambers of this Neolithic long barrow are now open to the elements, the whole structure was originally covered by a mound, the remains of which can still be traced. The interior is cross-shaped, a short gallery leading to an end chamber and with one chamber on each side, the internal length being only 19 feet (5.8 metres) (as compared, for example, with the 48-foot/14.6-metre passage inside Stoney Littleton burial chamber, described on page 69). The barrow has been excavated twice, and twenty to thirty burials were found, plus pottery, an arrowhead, flint flakes and bone tools. Some of the finds can be seen in Stroud Museum.

49

Notgrove chambered long barrow, Gloucestershire

This Neolithic tomb is a good example of what happens to a megalithic burial chamber which is excavated and then left open to the weather. When burial chambers are restored, a certain amount of rebuilding is necessary, and such unnatural materials as concrete are often used. This work can with some justification be criticised by the purist. But if the alternative is a sad picture of dereliction, such as we see at Notgrove, then surely preservation is justified. When the result is a beautiful structure like Belas Knap long barrow

not far away (see page 77), preservation is certainly justified.

The mound at Notgrove burial chamber, originally about 160 feet (48.8 metres) long and 80 feet (24.4 metres) wide, still contains the large stones which formed the interior gallery grave. They are now in a hollow in the centre of the mound, but would have originally been buried inside it. During excavation, the bones of several adults and children were discovered, along with animal bones, in the chambers. More bones were found in the forecourt. The excavators also found an earlier stone burial chamber in the mound, to the west of the gallery grave, and this contained the crouched skeleton of a man aged fifty to sixty.

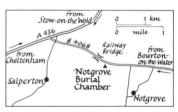

Map reference:
SP 096212 (metric map 163, 1-inch map 144)
Nearest town: Cheltenham
Nearest village: Notgrove
Location: The tomb is right beside the B4068 road about 11 miles (17.5 kilometres) east of Cheltenham. It is about 300 yards (274 metres) away from the railway bridge, and beside a track. There is a layby beside the main road. The site is in the care of the Department of the Environment, and is signposted.

50

Belas Knap chambered long barrow, Gloucestershire

Lying like a beached whale 1,000 feet (300 metres) up on the Cotswold hills, this Neolithic long barrow is an impressive sight and certainly justifies the long walk needed to reach it. The first feature you will see is the deeply indented forecourt, but this was built to mislead – it is not the entrance to the mound at all. Two upright stones with a lintel across the top form a false entrance blocked by another stone (see photograph below). Whether this elaborate false entrance was intended to foil

Map reference:
SP 021254 (metric map 163, 1-inch map 144)
Nearest town: Cheltenham
Nearest village: Winchcombe
Location: The path to Belas Knap leaves a minor road about 2 miles (3 kilometres) south of Winchcombe (which is itself 6 miles/9.5 kilometres north-east of Cheltenham). It is signposted 'Belas Knap 1 km', and opposite is a small layby. The path winds uphill round the field edges, but it is well signposted all the way. This is an exhilarating walk, with fine views, but can be muddy in wet weather. The barrow is in the care of the Department of the Environment.

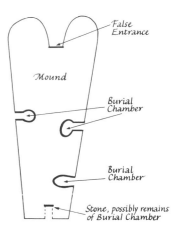

human tomb robbers or evil spirits, or whether it had some symbolic meaning, is not known.

The barrow is 60 feet (184 metres) wide and 13 feet (4 metres) high at this northern end, and there are four small burial chambers tucked away in the sides of its huge bulk, 180 feet (54.7 metres) long. Three of these chambers can be entered (see top photograph), but the fourth, at the southern end, may have been only a cist, for no more than one stone remains today. During excavations in 1863–5 and 1928–30, the bones of thirty people were found in the chambers, and behind the false entrance were more bones and a man's skull. The barrow was restored in 1930–1, and one particularly impressive feature is the drystone walling (the upper parts have been restored).

Looking south along the hillfort. (The car park can just be seen in the bottom left corner, and the main path up into the fort.)

51

Herefordshire Beacon hillfort, Hereford and Worcester

John Evelyn the diarist said that the view from the Beacon was 'one of the goodliest vistas in England', and we feel inclined to agree with him. On a fine day, the hill commands vast areas of hill and plain, the view along the spine of the Malvern Hills being especially memorable. But let us not be so overwhelmed by what lies beyond its defences that we neglect the fort itself. The Herefordshire Beacon hillfort rivals Maiden Castle in its beauty of line, as it lies draped sinuously around a ridge atop the Malverns. In its present state the fort covers 32 acres (13 hectares); the original third century BC enclosure covered a mere 8 acres (3.2 hectares) until it was enlarged later in the Iron Age. The impressive bank, ditch and counterscarp bank approximately follow the 1,000-foot contour around the hill, with entrances at the west, south, north-east and east. A ring-motte on the highest point dates from the eleventh or twelfth centuries AD, and a dyke along the crest of the hills was constructed by the Earl of Gloucester around 1287 to divide his territory from that of the Bishop of Hereford.

Map reference:
SO 760400 (metric map 150, 1-inch map 143)
Nearest town: Great Malvern
Nearest village: Malvern Wells
Location: The fort is in the southern part of the Malvern Hills, 3 miles (5 kilometres) south-west of Great Malvern and immediately south of the A449 road. There is a large car park opposite the British Camp Hotel. The path uphill is clearly marked, but rather steep.

The northern ramparts

52

**Arthur's Stone chambered tomb,
Hereford and Worcester**

The 'Arthur' of the name is of course King Arthur, and there are several versions of the tradition which involves him in the siting of this tomb. One is that a king who had a fight with him is buried here; another is that Arthur killed a giant who is buried here; a third tells that it is Arthur himself who is buried at this spot, his tomb marked by this impressive stone monument. In fact it is all that remains of a Neolithic chambered tomb. The burial chamber is roofed by a large capstone supported by nine upright stones, and a much ruined passageway 15 feet (4.6 metres) long can still be traced along its course to the chamber. The whole structure would have been covered by a mound.

Not far away to the south is a stone bearing small cup-marks, and these have several traditional interpretations: that they were made by the giant's elbows as he fell; that Arthur knelt on the stone to pray, and so made the holes; that they were made to take the heels of quoits players (thus giving the stone the name Quoit Stone).

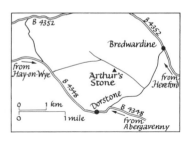

Map reference for Arthur's Stone:
SO 319431 (metric maps 148 & 161, 1-inch map 142)
Nearest town: Hay-on-Wye
Nearest village: Dorstone
Location: Arthur's Stone is right beside a lane to the north of Dorstone, which is itself in the attractive border countryside to the south of the River Wye and 5 miles (8 kilometres) east of Hay-on-Wye.

Map reference for Nordy Bank:
SO 576847 (metric maps 137 & 138, 1-inch map 129)
Nearest town: Ludlow
Nearest village: Clee St Margaret
Location: 7 miles (11 kilometres) north-east of Ludlow, Nordy Bank is close to a minor road just north of Clee St Margaret. Park near the gate with the notice 'No vehicles allowed. Footpath only', but leave the gateway clear. The fort is then a short walk away, through the gate and up the hillside ahead.

53

Nordy Bank hillfort, Salop

Deep in the heart of rural Salop, this compact Iron Age hillfort (4 acres/1.6 hectares) overlooks picturesque valley and hill scenery. A single bank and ditch form the defences, with an entrance at the north-west. (See page 80 for location details.)

The hillfort's outer bank can be seen running from the foreground into the middle distance and curving round to the right. The bank of low cloud in the background was making rapid progress down the hills towards us, soon to make photography impossible.

54

Old Oswestry hillfort, Salop

This impressive Iron Age hillfort lies immediately north of the town whose name it bears. Indeed there was a tradition in Oswestry that the hillfort was the original site of the town, which was then later moved ¾ mile (1 kilometre) south. There may be some truth in that because pre-war excavations at the fort have shown that it was occupied from the third century BC until the Roman period, the inhabitants living first in circular wood huts and later in dwellings with thick stone walls.

The development of the defences into what we see today seems to have gone through three or more phases, and in each phase different banks and ditches were dug. These ramparts are still impressive, as the photograph shows.

Old Oswestry is not far from the Welsh border. The linear earthwork known as Wat's Dyke was built in the early eighth century AD to delineate the boundary between Wales and Mercia, some years before the construction of the more famous Offa's Dyke which superseded it, and Wat's Dyke touches Old Oswestry to north and south. Old Oswestry has very slight Arthurian connections in that its traditional name was Caer Ogyrfan or Gogyrfan's fort, Gogyrfan being Guinevere's father, but A.H.A. Hogg in his *Hill-Forts of Britain* warns us not to take this association too seriously: 'in view of the revised dating of the coarse pottery associated with the latest occupation [it has now been recognised as Iron Age rather than post-Roman as was originally thought] one must now regretfully abandon the romantic vision of King Arthur riding through the ruins of the great west entrance to visit his future in-laws.'

Map reference:
SJ 295310 (metric map 126, 1-inch map 118)
Nearest town: Oswestry
Location: Old Oswestry is only ¾ mile (1 kilometre) north of the town, and is reached along a lane off the A483 road. It is signposted at the main road and there is room to park opposite the entrance gate. The fort is in the care of the Department of the Environment.

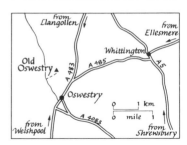

Old Oswestry, 'the outstanding work of Early Iron Age type on the Marches of Wales' (Sir Cyril Fox).

Map reference:
SJ 044128 (metric map 128, 1-inch map 120)
Nearest town: Rugeley
Nearest village: Cannock Wood
Location: The fort is 3 miles (5 kilometres) due south of Rugeley and most easily approached from the south, via Cannock Wood, where it is signposted. There is a car park opposite the Park Gate Inn, and immediately beyond the car park is the first line of ramparts. The fort is maintained by Cannock Chase District Council.

55

Castle Ring hillfort, Staffordshire

Castle Ring is at the highest point in Cannock Chase (an attractive area of forest and heath land), 801 feet (244 metres) above sea level, and is an Iron Age hillfort of 8¼ acres (3.4 hectares). It is five-sided, and the defences vary from two banks and ditches with a counterscarp bank on the north and west, to five banks and four ditches on the south and south-east where the ground is flatter. The original entrance is on the east.

Though this was probably once a remote spot (and it is certainly still attractive), 'civilisation' has encroached and it is now a popular local beauty spot, much visited at weekends and holidays. Consequently if you prefer peace and quiet, choose some other time for your visit. One scar of modern Britain which you will be unable to avoid, however, is the power station seen lurking through the pine trees in the direction of Rugeley.

56

Burrough Hill hillfort, Leicestershire

The rural delights of east Leicestershire are spread out below for inspection from the summit of Burrough Hill, a popular local beauty spot. A strong rampart and ditch enclose around 12 acres (5 hectares) to form an Iron Age hillfort with a prominent entrance breaking the ramparts. Excavation at this entrance revealed traces of a cobbled roadway and a guard house with strong masonry walls. Finds have been of a domestic nature – horse, sheep, cow and pig bones, querns for grinding grain, and pottery – and the excavations have shown that the site was occupied for several centuries. It may have been the capital of the Coritani, the tribe that once ruled this area of the Midlands, but there is no real evidence to support this theory.

After the abandonment of the settlement in Roman times, the fort still remained an important place, with fairs and festivals being held there, and a quotation from the sixteenth-century antiquarian John Leland illustrates how the site continued to be used: 'To these Borowe hills every year on Monday after White Sunday, com people of the country thereabouts, and shoote, runne, wrestle, dance, and use other feats of like exercise.' Although this practice died out in the eighteenth century, the fort is still used for playing games today, and people exercise their horses there as well as their dogs. Indeed, the Grand National was held there in 1873, and the fort has also been used for steeple-chasing.

Although Burrough Hill is a pleasant place in summer, it can be bleak and inhospitable in winter, as the following story shows. During the last century, a village schoolmaster was lost there in a snowstorm, and when his violin was found two days later it was feared he had perished. However next day a search party found him in the snow, amazingly little the worse for wear.

The well-defined entrance

Map reference:
SK 758119 (metric map 129, 1-inch map 122)
Nearest town: Melton Mowbray
Nearest village: Burrough on the Hill
Location: 5 miles (8 kilometres) south of
Melton Mowbray, Burrough Hill is best
approached from the south, along the lane
between Burrough on the Hill and Somerby.
At the sharp bend, a gateway leads into a field
used as a car park, and from there it is a walk
of 600 yards (550 metres) to the hillfort. The
path can be muddy in wet weather.

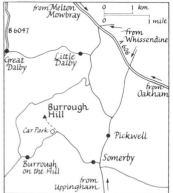

57

Warham Camp, Norfolk

This is an impressive plateau fort in a part of Britain where prehistoric sites worth seeing are few and far between. Thought to have been constructed by the Iceni at the end of the first century BC or early in the first century AD, the ramparts (still over 8 or 9 feet/2 metres high) contain an area of 3½ acres (1.4 hectares). There are no ramparts to the south-west; this is a result of eighteenth-century landscaping when the adjoining river course was changed and a bank and ditch removed in the process. It is not clear which of the entrances are original. Some are thought to have been made about 100 years ago when trees were removed from the fort.

See page 87 top right for location details.

58

Honington Camp, Lincolnshire

Hillforts are an unusual sight in Lincolnshire, and indeed Honington Camp can scarcely be called a 'hill' fort because it stands on no more than a slight plateau above the surrounding countryside. However its internal area of 1 acre (.5 hectare) is well defended by double banks and ditches with a counterscarp bank, and there is one entrance on the east. Although apparently an Iron Age fort, Roman coins were found there in the seventeenth century.

Map reference for Warham Camp:
TF 944409 (metric map 132, 1-inch map 125)
Nearest town: Wells-next-the-Sea
Nearest village: Warham St Mary
Location: 3 miles (5 kilometres) south-east of Wells-next-the-Sea, Warham Camp is right beside the River Stiffkey, on its eastern bank, and a bridle path leads to it from the lane running north–south between Warham St Mary and Wighton.

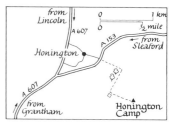

Map reference for Honington Camp:
SK 954423 (metric map 130, 1-inch map 113)
Nearest town: Grantham
Nearest village: Honington
Location: The camp is on farmland on a rise 1 mile (1.5 kilometres) to the south-east of Honington, and 4½ miles (7 kilometres) north-east of Grantham. It is reached along a track off the A153 road, and how far you drive along the track really depends on you and your vehicle. Follow the route as shown on the sketch map, for on the Ordnance Survey map which we have (1 inch to 1 mile, no. 113, fully revised 1960–61) the footpath is shown in the wrong place.

59

Stanton Moor cairns,
Nine Ladies stone circle, and the King Stone,
Derbyshire

In fine weather a walk across Stanton Moor is rewarded by lovely views across the surrounding countryside, as well as by the sight of several prehistoric remains. The moor, a sandstone plateau of 150 acres (60 hectares), seems to have been used as a burial ground during the Early Bronze Age, for the remains of around seventy **cairns** have been found. Several of them are close by the path leading to the stone circle, and can be easily examined. (They have all been numbered in the past, and we shall use these numbers to identify them in this description and on the sketch map.)

T36 A stone battle-axe and the cremated remains of a woman were found in this small cairn.

T2 This large cairn still stands 5 feet (1.5 metres) high, though a large part of the mound has gone. The stone burial cist which can be seen in the centre contained a cremated boy together with broken pottery and bronze fragments. There were over a dozen other burials in the mound itself, accompanied by pottery vessels and flint tools.

T43 This is a ring cairn, a low circular bank of stones about 59 feet (18 metres) across which enclosed a small burial mound.

T55 Another large but damaged cairn.

Some of the finds from Stanton Moor are in the Heathcote Museum at Birchover and can be seen by appointment (write to the Heathcote Museum, Birchover, Matlock, DE4 2BN, or ring Winster 313).

The **Nine Ladies** is a small and compact stone circle of nine stones, the tallest of which is only 3 feet 3 inches (1 metre) above the ground. The circle's diameter is around 36 feet (11 metres), and there used to be the remains of a cairn in the centre. Not far away is the **King Stone**, a single standing stone 3 feet (.9 metre) high, and it is recorded that as late as the end of the eighteenth century there were at least three more stone circles in the vicinity. The 'Nine Ladies' are traditionally

The cist in cairn T2

said to have been a group of women who were turned to stone for dancing on the Sabbath. Their fiddler was also petrified, in this case presumably the King Stone. This same story is told of a number of stone circles in the British Isles, sometimes with amusing variations, and other examples of petrification in this guidebook include the Merry Maidens stone circle (page 16), the Hurlers stone circles (page 23, the Rollright Stones (page 50), and Stanton Drew stone circles (page 70).

Nine Ladies stone circle

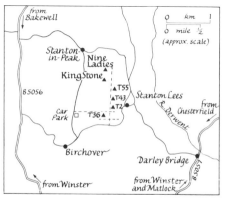

Map reference:
Nine Ladies
SK 249635 (metric map 119, 1-inch map 111)
Nearest town: Matlock
Nearest village: Birchover
Location: Stanton Moor is 3 miles (5 kilometres) north-west of Matlock. There are two main public entrances to the moor, both in the south near Birchover. That on the minor road to Stanton-in-Peak has a car park, but it is not always open. The other entrance is on the minor road to Stanton Lees, and Ministry signposts from Birchover will direct you here. From the road it is a walk of ¾ mile (1.2 kilometres) to the stone circle, which lies among the young birch trees to the left of the path, surrounded by a low stone wall. The Nine Ladies and the King Stone are in the care of the Department of the Environment, and a description of them is included in the guidebook to Arbor Low.

60

Nine Stones, Derbyshire

These four impressive stones on Harthill Moor are thought to be all that remains of a burial chamber. There were six stones in 1847 when the site was investigated.

The name 'Nine Stones' does not necessarily mean that there were once nine stones here. This name (and similar ones like Nine Maidens or Nine Ladies) was often given to stone circles where, it was traditionally believed, the stones were in the habit of dancing, usually at midday. 'Nine' really means 'noon', it has been suggested.

The stones on Harthill Moor do have a tradition of this kind. They were sometimes called the 'Grey Ladies', and were said to dance, not at midday but at midnight.

Colin shows the deep grooves in one of the stones. (See the Devil's Arrows, page 97, for similar grooving.)

Map reference:
SK 226626 (metric map 119, 1-inch map 111)
Nearest town: Bakewell
Nearest village: Elton
Location: 3 miles (5 kilometres) south of Bakewell, the stones can be seen from the minor road between Alport and Elton – they are about 300 yards (270 metres) from the road in an easterly direction, opposite a farm 1½ miles (2.5 kilometres) north of Elton. There is room to park off the road just north of the gateway and path leading to the stones.

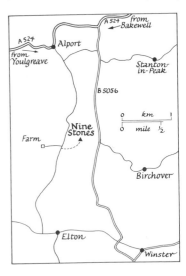

Arbor Low (see page 92). The Bronze Age tumulus can be seen in the foreground bank. On the left is the beginning of the earth bank adjoining the henge.

61

Arbor Low henge and Gib Hill tumulus, Derbyshire

A unique site located high up in Derbyshire's 'White Peak' (the limestone area of the Peak District), **Arbor Low** can be a bleak place in bad weather despite the fact that it is now surrounded by green fields rather than barren moorland. What antiquarian Thomas Bateman wrote in 1848 still applies today: 'Were it not for a few stone walls which intervene in the foreground, the solitude of the place and the boundless views are such as almost carry the observer back through a multitude of centuries and make him believe that he sees the same view and the same state of things as existed in the days of the architects of this once holy place.'

Looking somewhat like a huge terrestrial clockface when seen from above, Arbor Low is in fact a henge monument – a circular bank enclosing a ditch and central plateau, around the circumference of which are about fifty large stones, with four in the centre. The bank is 250 feet (76.5 metres) in diameter, and around 7 feet (2.1 metres) higher than the surrounding land; the ditch is on average 5½ feet (1.7 metres) deep today. The large limestone slabs within the henge are now recumbent (except for one, which is partly erect), and no one is sure whether they ever stood upright. No other site is known where the stones were laid flat when the monument was constructed, but that does not mean it could not have been so here. Perhaps a more likely explanation is that the stones were originally erect but were laid flat at a later time to 'de-sanctify' the site. This could have been done in distant times by people who understood the significance of these monuments and how they worked, and who knew that by performing this ritual they could de-activate the potency of Arbor Low. Or it could have been done much nearer our own times, by people who did not understand the practices of prehistoric peoples but distrusted and feared what they did not understand. Being inflamed with passion for the Christian religion, they consequently wished to ensure the demise of paganism, and by a ritual upheaval of the stones at Arbor Low they felt they were making the site safe. All this is sheer speculation. Although there is on record the statement of a local man living at the beginning of the eighteenth century who said he remembered seeing some of the stones standing, an attempt made by archaeologists at the beginning of this century to discover traces of socket-holes which could have supported the erect stones was completely unsuccessful. And so the question 'Were the stones at Arbor Low ever upright?' remains unanswered.

There have been several excavations at Arbor Low, the most recent being in 1901 and 1902, but no major finds of objects were made during investigations into the ditch, bank and plateau.

Right *Gib Hill seen from Arbor Low.*
Below *Some of the recumbent stones, with the tumulus in the background.*

Map reference:
SK 160636 (metric map 119, 1-inch map 111)
Nearest town: Bakewell
Nearest village: Middleton
Location: Arbor Low is 3 miles (5 kilometres) west of Middleton and 4½ miles (7 kilometres) south-west of Bakewell. It is approached from a minor road which runs close to it on the north. The site is signposted at the point where a farm track branches off the minor road, and a short distance along this track a rough sign requests that you park in the field alongside the track. A small entrance charge is payable at the farm, from where it is a short walk, well signposted, up to the henge. Gib Hill can be seen from the henge, and there is access to it via a stile in the stone wall. Both sites are in the care of the Department of the Environment, who have published a guidebook to these and three other Derbyshire sites.

Considerable archaeological attention has been paid to the tumulus which adjoins the bank at one point, and which was in fact constructed of material taken from the bank. (This tumulus is thought to have been built during the Bronze Age, somewhat later than the late Neolithic/Early Bronze Age date assigned to the henge.) Several people failed to find the burial, but Thomas Bateman was successful in 1845, when he located a limestone cist containing burnt human bones and two clay urns. The finds from all the excavations are now in the Sheffield, Buxton and British Museums.

The henge has two entrances, to the north-west and south-east, and close to the south-east entrance, in the field outside the bank, can be seen a low earth bank leading away from the henge.

Excavation has shown that this earthwork was built at the same time as the henge, so it is very unlikely to have connected Arbor Low with nearby **Gib Hill**, as has been suggested, because Gib Hill seems to have been constructed later, in the Bronze Age. It is possible to examine Gib Hill at close quarters, and despite several excavations it is still an impressive burial mound, standing around 16 feet (5 metres) high. Thomas Bateman found the burial cist in 1848, unexpectedly located near the top of the mound (they had been searching for it at the bottom). It contained a small urn and burnt human bones, and he had the whole cist removed to his garden. It has now been restored to its original place in the mound, though it is not now covered with earth as it would have been originally.

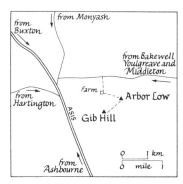

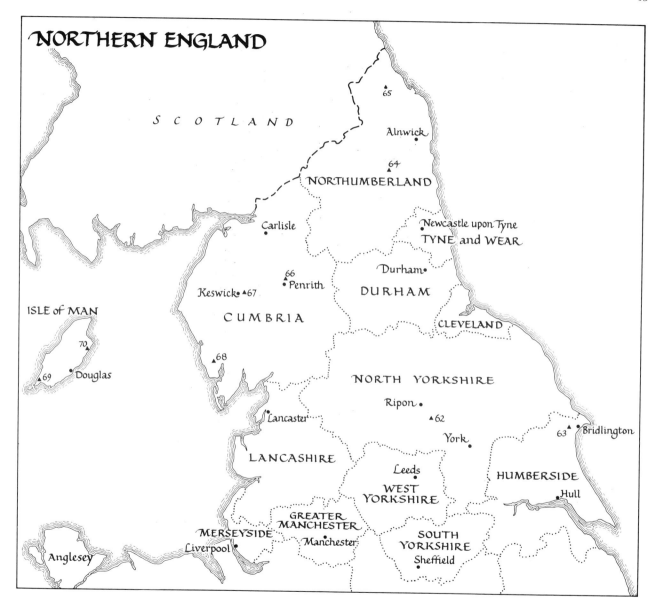

NORTHERN ENGLAND

SCOTLAND

●65

Alnwick●

●64
▲

NORTHUMBERLAND

Carlisle
●

Newcastle upon Tyne●
TYNE and WEAR

Durham●

66
▲
●Penrith

DURHAM

Keswick● ▲67

CUMBRIA

CLEVELAND

ISLE of MAN

70
▲

▲68

69
▲
●Douglas

NORTH YORKSHIRE

Ripon
●

▲62

●Lancaster

York
●

63 ▲●Bridlington

LANCASHIRE

Leeds
●

HUMBERSIDE

WEST
YORKSHIRE

●Hull

GREATER
MANCHESTER

MERSEYSIDE
●Manchester

SOUTH
YORKSHIRE

Liverpool●

Sheffield●

Anglesey

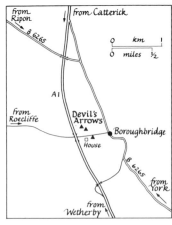

Map reference:
SE 391665 (metric map 99, 1-inch map 91)
Nearest town: Ripon
Nearest village: Boroughbridge
Location: The stones are close to the A1 road
(and as a result the constant noise from this
main road rather spoils the atmosphere of the
place). If you are approaching along the A1,
take the Boroughbridge turn-off and in the
village follow the lane to Roecliffe. On the
outskirts of Boroughbridge, just before the
lane goes under the A1, you will see two of
the Devil's Arrows in a field to your right; the
third is beside the road on your left, close to a
house and partly hidden in trees and
undergrowth. If you wish to examine the
stones from close to, take great care not to
disturb whatever crop is growing around
them. There is room to park in the field
gateway.

*In past centuries the St Barnabas Fair was held in a field between Boroughbridge and the Devil's Arrows,
and antiquarian William Stukeley suggested that the fair may have been the successor to ceremonies held at
the Devil's Arrows themselves in even earlier times.*

62

The Devil's Arrows, North Yorkshire

Three massive standing stones form an alignment 570 feet (174 metres) long in fields near Boroughbridge. They are 18 feet (5.5 metres), 21 feet (6.4 metres) and 22½ feet (6.8 metres) tall, and there were originally four stones, recorded as late as the sixteenth century by antiquarians Leland and Camden. Treasure-hunting down the centuries has damaged or destroyed many an important prehistoric site, and this seems to have been the fate of the missing Arrow, for Camden said in 1582 that it 'was lately pulled downe, by some that hoped though in vaine to find treasure'.

The stones take their name from a story told to explain their presence. The Devil was out to destroy the early Christian settlement at Aldborough and fired four 'arrows' from Howe Hill near Fountains Abbey, but, as often happened, his aim was poor and the missiles fell short. Whatever the origin of this story, it is certainly true that the stones were brought some distance. They are of millstone grit, quarried at Knaresborough some 6½ miles (10.5 kilometres) away. The prominent grooves at the top of the stones are generally thought to be the result of weathering. This explanation has been queried, and some people believe that the grooves were made by whoever erected the stones, for some unknown purpose. Other standing stones show the same feature, for example Nine Stones in Derbyshire (page 90).

63

Rudston monolith, Humberside

How long this standing stone has been here is not known, though informed opinion dates its erection to about the beginning of the Bronze Age, so perhaps it has stood for some 4,000 years. This indicates that the site was held sacred long before Christianity came to Britain. The first Christian church was built here just after the Norman

Conquest, the Christians taking over a site that had already been venerated for many generations.

The stone is now 25 feet 9 inches (7.8 metres) tall, but it looks as though the top has at some time been damaged, and originally it may have been 28 feet (8.5 metres) tall. Even now, it is the tallest standing stone in Britain. At its base the stone is roughly 6 feet (1.8 metres) by 3 feet (.9 metres), and it is said that there is as much below ground as can be seen above. The name 'Rudston' suggests that the stone may have once had a christianising cross head placed on top, as the Old English word *rood* means 'cross' and *stan* means 'stone'. The Christians frequently took over the existing pagan holy sites, built churches upon them, and carved crosses on or in some other way christianised the pagans' sacred stones.

The nearest source of this particular gritstone is some 10 miles (16 kilometres) away to the north at Cayton Bay or Cornelian Bay, and it must have taken considerable effort and ingenuity to move this massive block across the countryside. A local tradition accounts for its strange situation in the churchyard by saying that the Devil, intending to destroy the church, hurled this huge bolt at it, but fortunately he missed. Only just, though, because it stuck into the earth a mere 12 feet (3.6 metres) from the church wall. In the north-east corner of the churchyard is another stone, 3 feet (1 metre) tall, which once stood nearer to the monolith and was probably associated with it originally.

Rudston monolith

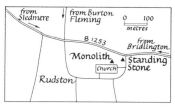

Map reference:
TA 098677 (metric map 101, 1-inch map 93)
Nearest town: Bridlington
Nearest village: Rudston
Location: The B1253 road passes through Rudston some 5 miles (8 kilometres) west of Bridlington. The church is beside this road, and the monolith is not easy to miss, as it towers high above the surrounding gravestones. A lane runs alongside the church and it is best to park somewhere along there, off the main road.

64

Lordenshaw hillfort and inscribed stones, Northumberland

Like most of the hillforts described in this book, Lordenshaw is impressively situated. High up in the lonely hills of Rothbury Forest, it overlooks some beautiful countryside, and although in itself not nearly as spectacular as southern forts like the Herefordshire Beacon or Maiden Castle, it has the added advantage that two interesting inscribed stones (one is illustrated right) can be examined on the way up to the fort. These two rock outcrops bear cup and ring marks, but that nearest the fort has unfortunately been mutilated by some ignorant person who thought the designs represented a map incorrectly drawn, and added an extra cup and ring mark!

The fort is small, covering just under an acre (.3 hectare), and the stony outer bank can still be traced, especially at the east entrance where the bank is broken (see photograph below). Inside the fort are the outlines of stone huts, probably dating from the Roman period. This means that three periods are represented here, for the carvings are probably Bronze Age, the hillfort Iron Age, and the hut sites Roman (i.e. built by natives living at the time of the Roman occupation).

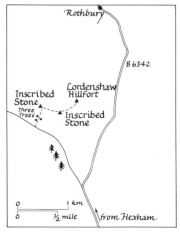

Map reference:
NZ 055993 (metric map 81, 1-inch map 71)
Nearest town: Alnwick
Nearest village: Rothbury
Location: The fort lies to the north of a lane 2 miles (3 kilometres) south of Rothbury (which is itself 11½ miles/18 kilometres south-west of Alnwick), and is reached by a walk of around 800 yards (730 metres). The route, and the position of the inscribed stones, are shown in detail on the sketch map. The point where the path leaves the road is not easy to locate in the open, featureless countryside, so you should look out for a group of three trees a short distance from the road on the righthand side, not far after the end of a plantation and approximately 1 mile (1.6 kilometres) from the B6342 road. There is plenty of room to park on the grass verge.

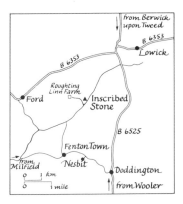

Map reference:
NT 984367 (metric map 75, 1-inch maps 64 & 71)
Nearest town: Berwick upon Tweed
Nearest village: Doddington
Location: The rock face is close to a lane about 3 miles (5 kilometres) to the north of Doddington and 9 miles (15 kilometres) south of Berwick. It cannot be seen from the road, and there is no signpost of any kind, so care needs to be exercised when locating it. Approaching the site from the north-east, it is approximately 2 miles (3 kilometres) along the lane from the B6525 road, and on the righthand side. It is in a clearing behind the gorse bushes and silver birch trees which form a small copse immediately to the north-east of the track leading to Roughting Linn Farm.

65

Roughting Linn inscribed stone, Northumberland

The subject of cup and ring marks, as these carvings are often called, is a highly controversial one. These truly enigmatic carvings have been found on a number of slabs of stone in the north of England, Scotland and Ireland, and although they are now well documented and have been much pondered over, their purpose and significance remain a complete mystery. There have, of course, been many interpretations of the variety of symbols recorded (maps of ancient sites; sacrificial symbols, the cups holding blood; primitive sundials; a game; mortars for grinding grains,

seeds, etc.; moulds used in metal casting; adder lairs; knife-sharpeners; mason's marks; lamps; writing; the signs of early metal prospectors; records of astronomical observations), but most are extremely unlikely and all have some flaw. Cup and ring marks and other designs have also been found carved on stones in chambered tombs and on standing stones, and several other examples will be found elsewhere in this book. Many other examples are described and the whole topic discussed in Evan Hadingham's book *Ancient Carvings in Britain*.

The carvings to be seen at Roughting Linn are among the best in the British Isles. A sloping rock slab 60 feet (18 metres) by 40 feet (12 metres) bears over sixty carvings in a variety of designs.

66

Long Meg and Her Daughters stone circle, Cumbria

This is an interesting Bronze Age site covering quite a large area. The stones are placed in an oval 360 feet (100 metres) by 305 feet (93 metres), and there were originally about seventy. Today there are fifty-nine, twenty-seven of them still standing. The stones of the circle are the daughters and Long Meg herself is a 12-foot (3.6 metres) standing stone just outside the circle (on the skyline in the photograph). On the flat surface of Long Meg that faces the circle are spiral carvings.

Tradition states that Long Meg and Her Daughters were a coven of witches who were holding their sabbat, some time in the thirteenth century. Michael Scot, a wizard from Scotland, found them so engaged and cast a spell over the assembled company, turning them all into stones. As with other circles, these stones are said to be uncountable, and if anyone can count them twice and arrive at the same total, the spell will be broken. It is also said that when a local squire attempted to remove the stones, a tremendous and terrifying storm broke out overhead and so the project was immediately abandoned. And finally, a prophecy tells us that if Long Meg were ever to be shattered, she would run with blood.

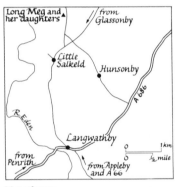

Map reference:
NY 571372 (metric map 91, 1-inch map 83)
Nearest town: Penrith
Nearest village: Little Salkeld
Location: 4 miles (6.5 kilometres) north-east of Penrith on the A686 road, a minor road leads north from Langwathby to Little Salkeld. ¼ mile (.5 kilometre) beyond Little Salkeld a track off to the left leads directly to the site, and there is room to park alongside the track.

Castlerigg stone circle (see page 102).

67

Castlerigg stone circle, Cumbria

Also known as the Keswick Carles, this nearly complete stone circle of thirty-eight stones with an average diameter of 100 feet (30 metres) is well worth a visit, not only to see the varied and fascinating shapes and textures of these ancient stones but also to admire the dramatic sensibility with which the people of the Bronze Age sited this sanctuary in what is, even today, one of the loveliest parts of Britain. The circle is, in effect,

within a natural amphitheatre formed by the surrounding hills, across which the shadows of the passing clouds make an ever-changing backdrop.

Nothing is really known about this site. In 1875 an unpolished stone axe was found here, and this is now in Keswick Museum. There was some excavation done in 1882 in the rectangular grouping of stones which joins on to the eastern side of the circle, but only charcoal was found. Of the thirty-eight stones five are now fallen and only a few are more than 5 feet (1.5 metres) high. (See page 103 top right for location details.)

Above *The stones of Swinside stone circle, sometimes known as Sunken Kirk, are said to be countless.*
Left *Some of the stones forming the rectangular group within Castlerigg stone circle.*

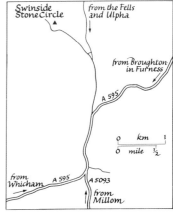

Map reference for Castlerigg:
NY 291236 (metric maps 89 & 90, 1-inch map 82)
Nearest town: Keswick
Location: The circle is 1½ miles (2.5 kilometres) east of Keswick. On the A66 road, a hundred yards east of its junction with the A591 road, a minor road leads south, and ¾ mile (1.2 kilometres) along this road the circle is in the centre of a field on the right. Look out for the National Trust noticeboard (the site is in the care of the National Trust and Department of the Environment). The road is wide enough to allow parking near the gate into the field.

Map reference for Swinside:
SD 172882 (metric map 96, 1-inch map 88)
Nearest town: Millom
Nearest village: Broughton in Furness
Location: 4 miles (6.5 kilometres) north of Millom the A595 road forms a Y junction with the A5093. ¾ mile (1 kilometre) further north on the A595 road, a minor road leads off north. ½ mile (.8 kilometre) along this minor road, a track off to the left (in a north-westerly direction) leads to Swinside Farm. ¾ mile (1 kilometre) along, the circle is on the right.

68

Swinside stone circle, Cumbria

This attractively compact circle of fifty-five stones dating from the Bronze Age is set out on the open fells and is about 90 feet (27 metres) in diameter. Excavation has revealed that the stones themselves have a foundation of a layer of packed pebbles to provide stability. There may have been an entrance at the south-east, as there are two outlying stones which suggest this.

69

The Meayll Circle chambered tomb, Isle of Man

The Mull Circle, Lhiack-ny-Wirragh (the stone of the meetings), and Rhullick-y-Lag-Sliggagh (the graveyard of broken slates) are alternative names for this site. Although marked on the Ordnance Survey map as a 'stone circle', it is in fact a Neolithic chambered tomb of unusual design. Six pairs of chambers built of stone slabs are arranged in a circle of approximately 50 feet (15 metres) diameter, and each pair has an entrance passage so that each structure is roughly T-shaped. Today they are roofless and project from a slight stony bank, but they were probably originally both roofed and covered by a mound. There may also have been a cist or burial chamber in the centre of the

One of the burial chambers

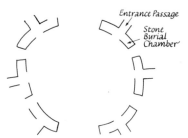

mound. During excavations in 1893, flints, arrowheads, a jet bead and pottery fragments were found in the chambers as well as cremated burials.

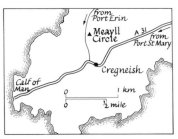

Map reference:
sc 189677 (metric map 95, 1-inch map 87)
Nearest town: Port Erin
Nearest village: Cregneish
Location: 1 mile (1.6 kilometres) south-west of Port Erin, the Meayll Circle is on a hilltop 100 yards (90 metres) east of the minor road from Port Erin to Cregneish.
   The visitor to the Isle of Man will find the booklet *Prehistoric Sites in the Isle of Man* (published by The Manx Museum and National Trust) of great interest and value.

An overall view of the Meayll Circle

Looking along the dilapidated burial chamber towards the standing stones at its entrance.

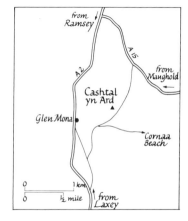

70

Cashtal-yn-Ard chambered tomb, Isle of Man

This Neolithic burial chamber would originally have been covered by a mound or cairn, but today most of this covering has disappeared, and the interior stones are exposed to public view and the depredations of the elements. The entrance was through a west-facing semi-circular forecourt and this is outlined by large stones. Some are the original stones unmoved, some are fallen stones re-erected, and some are new stones placed in identified holes. Behind the tall portal stones is a chamber 38 feet (11.5 metres) long, built of slabs of stone and divided into five compartments. When the site was excavated in 1935, nothing but flints and pottery fragments were found in the chamber. 11 feet (3.5 metres) behind the chamber a mound of burnt earth and stones was found.

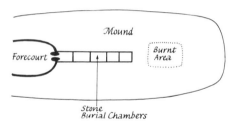

Map reference:
SC 462892 (metric map 95, 1-inch map 87)
Nearest town: Ramsey
Nearest village: Glen Mona
Location: Cashtal-yn-Ard is 3 miles (5 kilometres) south of Ramsey, in the parish of Maughold. A minor road links the A15 and A2 roads, and the track to Cashtal-yn-Ard leaves this minor road at a sharp double bend. Go through the gate, follow a track past a ruined cottage, along the edge of a field, and over a stile by a copse of fir trees. It sounds a long way, but is only about 200 yards (180 metres) from the road.
   The visitor to the Isle of Man will find the booklet *Prehistoric Sites in the Isle of Man* (published by The Manx Museum and National Trust) of great interest and value.

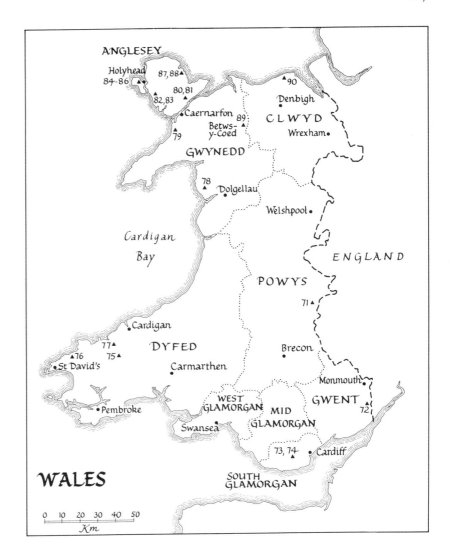

ANGLESEY

Holyhead
84-86 ▲
87,88 ▲
80,81 ▲
82,83 ▲
• Caernarfon
89 ▲
▲ 90
• Denbigh
C L W Y D
Betws-
y-Coed
Wrexham •
79 ▲
GWYNEDD

78 ▲
• Dolgellau

Welshpool •

Cardigan
Bay

E N G L A N D

P O W Y S

71 ▲

• Cardigan
77 ▲
75 ▲
D Y F E D
• Brecon
▲ 76
St David's
Carmarthen •

Monmouth •
GWENT
72 ▲

WEST
GLAMORGAN
MID
GLAMORGAN
• Pembroke

Swansea •
73, 74 ▲ • Cardiff

WALES

SOUTH
GLAMORGAN

0 10 20 30 40 50
Km

71

Four Stones, Radnor (Powys)

The Four Stones are a bit of a mystery, because no one seems to know much about them! It has been suggested that they are all that remains of a Bronze Age stone circle (though their formation does not really support this theory). They hold a place in local folklore, however, as the burial place of four kings killed in battle nearby, and it is said that every night (or when they heard the bells of Old Radnor church) the stones used to go down to the Hindwell Pool to drink. Traditions which credit standing stones with the power of mobility, and other human characteristics, are widespread – see our book *The Secret Country* for examples.

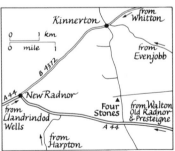

Map reference:
SO 246608 (metric map 148, 1-inch map 128)
Nearest town: Presteigne
Nearest village: Kinnerton
Location: The stones stand beside a minor road 1½ miles (2.5 kilometres) due south of Kinnerton and 6 miles (9.5 kilometres) south-west of Presteigne.

72

Harold's Stones, Monmouth (Gwent)

Three tall stones stand leaning at all angles in a field just outside the village of Trellech. Their purpose is unknown, and they may once have been part of a larger stone monument. Although they were said to commemorate a battle won by King Harold, they probably date from the Bronze Age. A folklore tradition tells how they were thrown down from the Sugar Loaf mountain by Jack o' Kent, a Herefordshire giant, when he was playing pitch and toss.

The stones are kept in good order by the local people, as also are two other interesting features in Trellech – Tump Terret, a steep, flat-topped mound incongruously located in a village farmyard (where those killed in the battle are said to be buried), and a healing well called the Virtuous Well or St Anne's Well, just outside the village. Also worth seeing are the ancient preaching cross in the churchyard, and the elegant seventeenth-century sundial now kept inside the church.

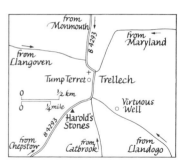

Map reference:
so 499051 (metric map 162, 1-inch map 155)
Nearest town: Monmouth
Nearest village: Trellech (often spelled 'Trelleck' on maps)
Location: Trellech is on the B4293 road, about 6 miles (9.5 kilometres) south of Monmouth. The stones are beside the road just to the south of the village; there is nowhere to park except on the road.

Harold's Stones are depicted on one of the faces of this sundial, dating from 1689, which can be seen inside Trellech church.

Left *The herringbone walling at the entrance to the burial chamber is a modern reconstruction.*
Right *The pit where corpses may have been left exposed.*

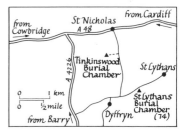

73

Tinkinswood chambered long cairn, Glamorgan (South Glamorgan)

At Tinkinswood (also known as Castell Carreg, Llech-y-Filiast, Maes-y-Filiast and Gwal-y-Filiast, names possibly connected with stories of King Arthur, which are widespread in Wales), the covering mound is still prominent (130 feet/40 metres long and 60 feet/18 metres wide). At one end is a burial chamber of large slabs, roofed by a huge capstone whose weight has been estimated at 40 tons (40 tonnes). Inside the chamber were found human bones, showing that at least fifty people were buried here in Neolithic times. Flints and pottery fragments were also found, and bones of sheep, pigs and oxen which may be the remains of funeral feasts.

In the mound itself, behind the capstone, a stone-lined pit can be seen, but its purpose is not

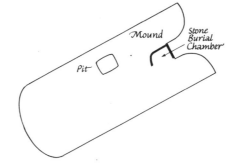

known. It has been suggested that corpses were left exposed in it before the skeletons were finally interred in the burial chamber.

It was once thought that to sleep at this site on the evenings preceding May Day, St John's Day or Midwinter Day would have dire consequences – the bold person who disregarded the warnings would either die, go mad, or become a poet!

Map reference:
ST 092733 (metric map 171, 1-inch map 154)
Nearest town: Barry
Nearest village: St Nicholas
Location: 4 miles (6.5 kilometres) north-west of Barry, Tinkinswood cairn is reached from a lane which leaves the A48 road at St Nicholas. It is signposted along the lane, about ¾ mile (1.2 kilometres) south of the village. There is no special parking area. A clearly signposted footpath of 400 yards (365 metres) leads across the fields to the cairn, which is in the care of the Department of the Environment. A leaflet describing this site and St Lythans cromlech is available.

74

St Lythans cromlech, Glamorgan (South Glamorgan)

In our tour through Wales we shall visit a number of cromlechs, similar in basic design to this one which still stands in unspoilt country surprisingly close to Cardiff. With each cromlech, several upright stones (in this instance, three) support a capstone, usually massive in dimensions and weight. That at St Lythans is 14 feet (4 metres) long, 10 feet (3 metres) wide, and 2½ feet (.7 metres) thick. We can only marvel at the skills of ancient man, who was able to position such blocks of stone by means of a technology, all knowledge of which has been lost.

There was once a mound of earth or stones covering this Neolithic burial chamber, but only slight traces remain. It is thought to have been similar to the surviving cairn at Tinkinswood not far away (see page 110). There are no excavation finds, but one nineteenth-century researcher recounted seeing bones and pottery mixed up with earth thrown out of the chamber.

Traditionally, the field in which the stones stand was said to be cursed, and consequently unprofitable, and the stones themselves were believed to grant any wish whispered to them on Hallowe'en.

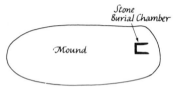

Map reference:
ST 101722 (metric map 171, 1-inch map 154)
Nearest town: Barry
Nearest village: Dyffryn
Location: 3 miles (5 kilometres) north-west of Barry, the cromlech stands in a field close beside the lane between Dyffryn and St Lythans. (See sketch map on page 110.) It is signposted, and there is room to park on the grass verge. The site is in the care of the Department of the Environment, who have published a leaflet describing it and also Tinkinswood cairn.

These gaunt, rugged stones are all that remains of St Lythans burial chamber, also known as Gwal-y-Filiast (the Greyhound Bitch's Lair – a name which may come from an Arthurian tale in the Mabinogion). The capstone is said to whirl round three times on Midsummer Eve, and the same night all the stones go to bathe in the river.

75

Gors Fawr stone circle, Pembroke (Dyfed)

On an expanse of moorland in the Preseli Mountains (where Stonehenge's bluestones came from) is a Bronze Age circle (above) of small stones 72 feet (22 metres) in diameter. Sixteen stones remain, and a short distance away to the north-east are two taller standing stones (top right) probably associated with the circle.

Map reference:
SN 135294 (metric map 145, 1-inch map 139)
Nearest town: Cardigan
Nearest village: Mynachlog-ddu
Location: The circle is not far from a minor road to the west of the A478 road, and it is signposted on the minor road. There is room to park on the grass verge by the gate, and from there it is a short walk of no more than 200 yards (180 metres) across the moor to the circle. In wet weather the ground is inclined to be marshy.

76

Carreg Samson cromlech, Pembroke (Dyfed)

Another impressive cromlech of the type which is so familiar in Wales and also in Cornwall, Carreg Samson used to be part of a field bank but now stands in splendid isolation, dominating a view of the bay and Strumble Head. The capstone is supported on three of the seven upright stones, and the whole structure was once a Neolithic burial chamber covered by a mound of earth or stones.

Enterprising people have sometimes found new uses for structures of this kind. Earlier this century stones were used to block the holes in the sides of this tomb and it was used as a sheep-shelter.

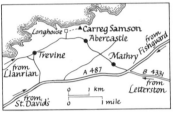

Map reference:
SM 848335 (metric map 157, 1-inch map 138/151)
Nearest town: Fishguard
Nearest village: Trevine
Location: Carreg Samson is 7 miles (11 kilometres) south-west of Fishguard, among the lanes north of the A487 road between Fishguard and St David's. The drive to Longhouse Farm branches off the lane between Trevine and Abercastle, and Carreg Samson is signposted here. You can either leave your car in the lane or drive to the farm, then taking care to park where you will not obstruct the farm business. Carreg Samson is now a short walk (200 yards/180 metres) away, through the gate and in the direction of the bay. It is in the care of the Department of the Environment.

Map reference:
SH 099370 (metric map 145, 1-inch map 139)
Nearest town: Cardigan
Nearest village: Brynberian
Location: 7 miles (11 kilometres) south-west of Cardigan, Pentre Ifan is tucked away in the lanes north of Brynberian, but the inexperienced map-reader need not worry, because the site is well signposted in the area. There is just about room to park in the lane, and the short footpath to the cromlech (100 yards/90 metres) is clearly indicated. The site is in the care of the Department of the Environment, who have published a leaflet describing Pentre Ifan and also other megalithic monuments in North Pembrokeshire.

77

Pentre Ifan cromlech, Pembroke (Dyfed)

A large and elegant capstone delicately balanced high above the ground on pointed supporting slabs is the dominant feature of this site, possibly the best-known prehistoric monument in Wales. The capstone is in fact 16½ feet (5 metres) long and 8 feet (2.5 metres) above the ground, and originally formed the roof of a Neolithic burial chamber. All was covered by a mound or cairn 130 feet (40 metres) long, of which traces still remain.

Fairies were sometimes to be seen here; they were described as resembling 'little children in clothes like soldiers' clothes and with red caps'.

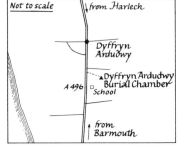

Map reference:
SH 589229 (metric map 124, 1-inch map 116)
Nearest town: Barmouth
Nearest village: Dyffryn Ardudwy
Location: The cairn is at the southern end of the village of Dyffryn Ardudwy, just behind the school, and a path leads directly to it from the main A496 road, where the site is clearly signposted. There is room to park in an adjoining side road. The site is in the care of the Department of the Environment, who have published a leaflet describing it.

78

Dyffryn Ardudwy chambered cairn, Merioneth (Gwynedd)

This important Neolithic monument is unusual in that it has two separate megalithic burial chambers. Now that their covering cairn of stones has almost disappeared (though archaeologists cannot be absolutely certain that the chambers were ever completely covered), they stand exposed 28 feet (8.6 metres) apart on a bed of white boulders. The smaller western chamber was built first, possibly in the mid third millennium BC, and surrounded by a small cairn; the larger eastern chamber, 12 feet (3.4 metres) long, dates from only a short time later, and a new cairn was built to include both chambers. Few finds have been made, because the site was disturbed in past centuries, but pottery fragments, traces of cremation burials, and two stone pendants were found and are in the National Museum of Wales in Cardiff.

79

Dinas Dinlle hillfort, Merioneth (Gwynedd)

The defences (two banks with a ditch between) surrounding this 3½-acre (1.4 hectares) hillfort can still be traced, especially to the east, but on the western side the site is being worn away by the sea. The fort cannot have been very far from the cliff edge when it was constructed, and one wonders what the people who lived there thought of the spectacular view which was always before them. The historians would have us believe that our ancestors' main concern was with food-gathering and other basic chores, but we do not doubt that they were at least as sensitive as people today to the beauties of nature. Maybe they even chose this site because of the view – who knows? We do not even know who 'they' were. Christopher Houlder tells us in *Wales: An Archaeological Guide* that the form and position of the fort 'suggest a beach-head fortification of Iron Age B immigrants', but adds that pottery and coins found there date from 500–600 years later, the second and third centuries AD.

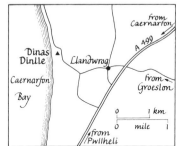

Map reference:
SH 437563 (metric maps 115 & 123, 1-inch maps 106 & 115)
Nearest town: Caernarfon
Nearest village: Llandwrog
Location: Dinas Dinlle is 4½ miles (7 kilometres) south-west of Caernarfon, and overlooks Caernarfon Bay. Minor roads lead to it from the A499 road, and when you reach the coast, you have arrived at the hillfort. Park on the pebbles by the Marine Cafe, and it is a short but steep climb up the grassy slope to the fort.

The surviving inland banks

80

**Bryn-Celli-Ddu chambered cairn,
Anglesey (Gwynedd)**

Anglesey is rich in prehistoric remains, many of which are well preserved and accessible. The first stop on our circular tour of the island is Bryn-Celli-Ddu, 'the Mound in the Dark Grove', the most interesting and impressive passage grave in Wales. Excavation has shown that there was originally a henge monument on the site, complete with ditch, bank, and circle of standing stones. This was probably constructed around 2000 BC; shortly afterwards the henge was destroyed and a burial cairn erected. An unusual feature of the site is a pit at the centre of the mound, just beyond the actual burial chamber. This pit may have been dug before the cairn was built, and contained wood and a human ear-bone. A carved stone found lying close by is now in the National Museum of Wales in Cardiff, but a cast has been erected beside the pit. It bears a zigzag, mazelike pattern on both faces and across the top (which can just be discerned on the cast), and this pattern may have been intended as a symbolic protection, in that only an initiate would be able to find his way through the maze. As with other prehistoric carvings, some of which are illustrated elsewhere in this book, the real meaning is unknown and will probably remain so. We are now too far away in time and attitude to be able to comprehend the significance of prehistoric ritual.

The passage grave was built of large stones, and consists of a passage 27 feet (8.2 metres) long and 3 feet (.9 metres) wide leading to a burial chamber 7–10 feet (2–3 metres) across and 6 feet (1.8 metres) high. A tall, smooth pillar (purpose unknown) stands in the chamber. The whole structure was covered by a mound, but the mound we see today has purposely been kept small so that the central pit and two stones which still survive from the henge can be seen.

Bones and flint tools were found during the first excavation in 1865, and a flint arrowhead and tools, shells, a stone bead and a scraper were found in 1929.

The entrance to the burial chamber

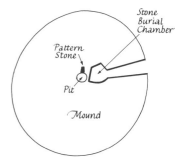

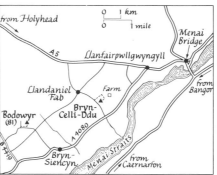

Map reference:
SH 508702 (metric maps 114 & 115, 1-inch maps 106 & 107)
Nearest town: Menai Bridge
Nearest village: Llanddaniel Fab
Location: The tomb is in fields close to a farm, and is approached along the lane leading to the farm. The lane joins a minor road about halfway between Llanddaniel Fab and the main A4080 road, so anyone who has just crossed the Menai Bridge on to Anglesey should head in a south-westerly direction for about 4 miles (6.5 kilometres) and at the crossroads turn right towards Llanddaniel Fab. The tomb is signposted along this lane, and there is also a notice requesting visitors to leave their cars at the road and walk the 800 yards (700 metres) to the monument. This is in the care of the Department of the Environment, and is kept unlocked during standard hours. A leaflet is available.

Left *Inside the burial chamber, looking back towards the entrance.*
Above *The pit in the centre of the mound, with the patterned stone.*

81

Bodowyr cromlech, Anglesey (Gwynedd)

The massive stones of this Neolithic burial chamber support a capstone measuring 8 feet (2.5 metres) by 6 feet (1.8 metres), and the whole structure would presumably once have been covered by a mound of earth or stones. The site has not been excavated, but it is one of a number of similar structures on the island of Anglesey, three of which are described in this book.

Map reference:
SH 462682 (metric maps 114 & 115, 1-inch map 106)
Nearest town: Menai Bridge
Nearest village: Llangaffo
Location: The cromlech is close to a minor road 1 mile (1.6 kilometres) east of Llangaffo and 7 miles (11 kilometres) south-west of Menai Bridge. The most direct approach is along a minor road which leaves the A4080 road a short distance to the west of Bryn-Siencyn. From this point it is a 1¼-mile (2 kilometres) drive to the site, which is signposted. Park on the grass verge and walk round the field edge (100 yards/90 metres) to the cromlech, which is in the care of the Department of the Environment. (See sketch map on page 119.)

82

Barclodiad-y-Gawres chambered cairn, Anglesey (Gwynedd)

The Welsh name of this Neolithic round cairn can be translated as 'The Giantess's Apronful', which refers to an old tradition, told in connection with a number of other sites throughout Britain, that they were formed by a giantess dropping an apronload of stones she was carrying around for some unspecified building project. The mound at

Barclodiad-y-Gawres is no longer of stones, the original cairn having been removed. The burial chamber is now covered by a modern concrete dome, built to protect the rare carved stones discovered there. The interior of the cairn is cross-shaped, a passage leading to a central burial chamber with three chambers leading off it. That on the right (west) side still has several upright slabs at its entrance: these would have been used to close it off. Cremated bones and broken bone pins have been found, and a hearth containing the bones of reptiles, fishes and small mammals.

Map reference:
SH 329707 (metric map 114, 1-inch map 106)
Nearest town: Holyhead
Nearest village: Rhosneigr
Location: 9 miles (14.5 kilometres) south-east of Holyhead, Barclodiad-y-Gawres is one of the most beautifully sited cairns, standing almost on the cliff top overlooking the bay of Trecastell on the south-west coast of Anglesey. The A4080 road passes close by; 2 miles (3 kilometres) north-west of Aberffraw it passes a sandy beach and car park. Leave your car here and walk along the path 500 yards (460 metres) to the tomb (signposted). It is in the care of the Department of the Environment, and open during standard hours. A leaflet is available.

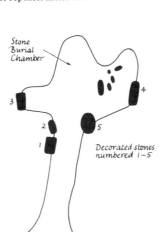

Decorated stones numbered 1–5

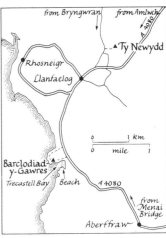

But the most important feature of Barclodiad-y-Gawres is the decorated stones. Five stones are carved to a greater or lesser degree, stone 5 on the plan being the most impressive and immediately noticeable (see photograph). Stone 4 has slight traces of a spiral and cupmark; stone 3 has several spirals; stone 2 has concentric circles and a lozenge at bottom right; and stone 1 has a weathered pattern of zigzags and lozenges. Some of these designs are similar to those carved on stones in Irish chambered tombs.

Overleaf *The grass-covered cairn overlooking the bay.*

Barclodiad-y-Gawres chambered cairn

83

Ty Newydd cromlech, Anglesey (Gwynedd)

Three uprights support a capstone 12 feet (3.6 metres) by 5 feet (1.5 metres), and excavation has shown that this Neolithic burial chamber was used into the Bronze Age – an arrowhead, pottery fragments and many pieces of white quartz, all of probable Bronze Age date, having been found there. As with many of these megalithic cromlechs, the earth covering has long since dispersed or been removed.

Map reference:
SH 344738 (metric map 114, 1-inch map 106)
Nearest town: Holyhead
Nearest village: Llanfaelog
Location: Ty Newydd is 7½ miles (12 kilometres) south-east of Holyhead and only ¾ mile (1.2 kilometres) north-east of Llanfaelog, and is reached along a minor road branching off the A4080 road. (See sketch map on page 121.) The path to the site (signposted) leaves the road at a sharp bend, and it is safest to park on the grass verge. It is only a short walk (100 yards/90 metres) across the field to the cromlech, which is in the care of the Department of the Environment.

84

Trefignath burial chamber, Anglesey (Gwynedd)

There are three interesting and easily accessible sites on Holyhead Island to the south and west of the town, the most unhappily sited being Trefignath Neolithic burial chamber. Today the outskirts of Holyhead are an industrial wasteland, and Trefignath overlooks an aluminium reduction plant. However if you can block this from view and concentrate on the burial chamber and its immediate surroundings, you will see an unusual structure of many stones, some tumbled, but the two 'portal' stones standing 7 feet (2 metres) high. A stone-built passageway 45 feet (13.7 metres) long was once divided into several chambers, but now that the protective earth mound has gone, the structure has become vulnerable to weathering. It was said that when the earth was removed, urns and human bones were found inside.

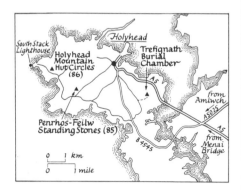

Map reference:
SH 260804 (metric map 114, 1-inch map 106)
Nearest town: Holyhead
Location: The burial chamber is 1½ miles (2.5 kilometres) south-east of the centre of Holyhead, beside a lane off and running parallel to the B4545 road. The site is signposted; park in the gateway and it is a short walk of 100 yards (90 metres) to the stones, which are in the care of the Department of the Environment.

Looking along the ruined burial chambers towards the portal stones.

85

**Penrhos-Feilw standing stones,
Anglesey (Gwynedd)**

These two shapely standing stones, 10 feet (3 metres) tall, are in a beautiful moorland setting. They are thought to date from the Bronze Age, but their significance has long since been forgotten.

Map reference:
SH 227809 (metric map 114, 1-inch map 106)
Nearest town: Holyhead
Location: The stones are 1½ miles (2.5 kilometres) south-west of Holyhead, in a field beside a minor road and behind a farm. (See sketch map on page 124.) They are signposted; park on the grass verge and go through the gate and across the field (only 100 yards/90 metres). The stones are in the care of the Department of the Environment.

86

**Holyhead Mountain hut circles,
Anglesey (Gwynedd)**

On the slope of Holyhead Mountain are the remains of around twenty circular and rectangular huts in an area of 15–20 acres (6–8 hectares). Over fifty huts were recorded in 1865. They are thought to have been occupied at the end of the Iron Age and into the Roman period, and finds include querns for grinding grain, spindle whorls, coins, and pottery from the third to fourth centuries AD. Copper slag found in one rectangular hut indicates that there was a metal-worker in residence. The name 'Cytiau Gwyddelod', or Irishmen's (Goidels') huts, is often used in connection with sites similar to this, but there is no evidence that they were occupied by the Irish.

As the remains consist of low stone walls (some of the huts also have discernible central hearths), they quickly become submerged once the bracken starts to grow, so it is advisable to visit this site during the winter or early spring.

Map reference:
SH 212820 (metric map 114, 1-inch map 106)
Nearest town: Holyhead
Location: The site is 2 miles (3 kilometres) west of Holyhead, not far from the South Stack lighthouse. The road leading to the lighthouse passes the site, which is sign-posted. (See sketch map on page 124.) There is a large car park immediately opposite the site, and from the road it is only a short walk through the bracken to the huts which are dotted around so that you come across them unexpectedly. The site is in the care of the Department of the Environment.

87

Din Lligwy settlement, Anglesey (Gwynedd)

The well-preserved remains of two circular and seven rectangular huts can be seen in an area of half an acre (.2 hectare), enclosed by the remains of a limestone wall. Some of the hut walls are still 6 feet (1.8 metres) high. Hearths in two of the rectangular buildings indicate that iron smelting took place there, and this native settlement has been dated to the fourth century AD, during the time of the Roman occupation of Britain.

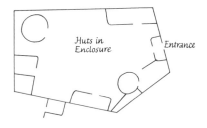

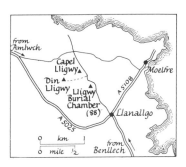

Map reference:
SH 497861 (metric map 114, 1-inch map 106)
Nearest town: Amlwch
Nearest village: Llanallgo
Location: Din Lligwy is not far from the east coast of Anglesey, and is 6 miles (9.5 kilometres) south-east of Amlwch. The A5025 road passes quite close to the site, but it is best approached from a minor road north of Llanallgo, and it is signposted on the lane. There is a layby for parking, and the 500-yard (450 metres) footpath through fields and woods to the site is clearly indicated. You will notice a ruined building to your right as you follow the footpath. This is Capel Lligwy, a twelfth to sixteenth-century chapel, which is worth the slight detour needed to visit it. Both Din Lligwy and Capel Lligwy are in the care of the Department of the Environment.

One of the best preserved circular huts

88

Lligwy cromlech, Anglesey (Gwynedd)

The gigantic capstone of this cromlech weighs about 28 tons (28 tonnes). Resting on small stones, it covers a hollow in the rock beneath, which was the burial chamber. Excavations in 1908 revealed human and animal bones, pottery, and mussel shells, and it is thought that the tomb was used by both Neolithic and Bronze Age peoples.

Map reference:
SH 501860 (metric map 114, 1-inch map 106)
Nearest town: Amlwch
Nearest village: Llanallgo
Location: The cromlech is just along the lane from the layby for Din Lligwy settlement, so visitors who have seen Din Lligwy should watch out for the sign to Lligwy cromlech as they continue southwards along the lane. Visitors coming from the south will see the cromlech on the lefthand side of the road just before they reach Din Lligwy. (See sketch map on page 127.) It is advisable to park on the grass verge in this narrow lane. The cromlech is in the care of the Department of the Environment.

89

Capel Garmon chambered long cairn, Denbigh (Gwynedd)

The Neolithic chambered tomb at Capel Garmon has been well preserved: careful restoration in the 1920s, after centuries of deterioration, has meant that the interesting features of this site can be easily examined. The interior of the tomb is now open to the sky, except for the western burial chamber which is covered by a large capstone 14 feet (4.3 metres) long. Originally of course the whole stone structure would have been roofed

with large stones, and all covered by a mound of earth or stones. On the eastern side of the mound was a false entrance (as at Belas Knap – see page 77). The real entrance to the chamber was along

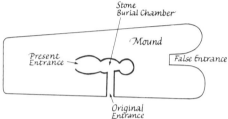

Map reference:
SH 818543 (metric map 116, 1-inch map 107)
Nearest town: Betws-y-Coed
Nearest village: Capel Garmon
Location: 1½ miles (2.5 kilometres) south-east of Betws-y-Coed, a minor road passes through Capel Garmon village, and ½ mile (.8 kilometre) to the south-east of the village a track leads from the road to a farm. The tomb is signposted by the road at this point. You can drive down the track and park on the grass verge before reaching the farm. The path to the tomb is signposted across a field, and it is only a short walk. The site is in the care of the Department of the Environment, who have published a leaflet.

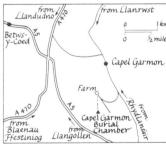

*Inside the cairn,
looking towards the roofed burial
chamber.*

a 15-foot (4.6 metres) passage on the southern side. Today this entrance is blocked off, and the visitor goes in through the western burial chamber, under the capstone. The reason for this is that during the last century the roofed chamber was used as a stable and an entrance was made directly into it.

Very little has been found in the tomb, due to earlier disturbance, apart from some fragments of pottery, bones and flints, but a number of small pieces of white quartz were found scattered around the forecourt area in front of the false entrance.

White quartz pebbles have been found at other burial sites, and stone circles and individual standing stones often contain a certain amount of quartz. The usual explanation for this is that quartz had a 'magical or religious significance' for prehistoric man, but we suspect that quartz may have had a more positive use, possibly in connection with the functioning of 'earth currents'. The theories are too complex to be explained here, but both 'earth currents' and quartz are discussed more fully in our book *The Secret Country*.

90

The Gop cairn, Flint (Clwyd)

This little-known mound, also called Gop-y-Goleuni barrow, is the second largest barrow in the British Isles, surpassed only by Silbury Hill – if that hill really *is* a barrow, which has not yet been proved. The Gop cairn is now approximately 40 feet (12 metres) high and there is an indentation on top showing where a shaft was sunk in 1886, but the excavators found only a few ox and horse bones. We wonder if, like Silbury Hill, the Gop cairn would continue to puzzle the archaeologists if it were further excavated, or would it soon reveal an important burial? The cairn's impressive hilltop position is shown in the photograph, taken with a telephoto lens from over a mile away.

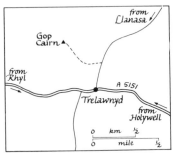

Map reference:
SJ 087802 (metric map 116, 1-inch map 108)
Nearest town: Prestatyn
Nearest village: Trelawnyd
Location: The cairn is on the hill above Trelawnyd, 1½ miles (2.5 kilometres) south-east of Prestatyn, and a path (500 yards/450 metres) leads to it from the village. A minor road leads north from the main A5151 road through the village, and a very short distance up this minor road, before reaching the first bend and the hill, a public footpath is signposted to the left, among the houses. There is room to park in the surrounding streets. Follow the path towards the double garage and beyond it over a stone stile. Strike diagonally uphill through the gorse bushes, and soon you should see the cairn above you on the hilltop. Take care when climbing to the top of the cairn because its sides are steep. There is a fine view from the top; the quarry which can be seen to the south-west is eating away the hillfort Moel Hiraddug.

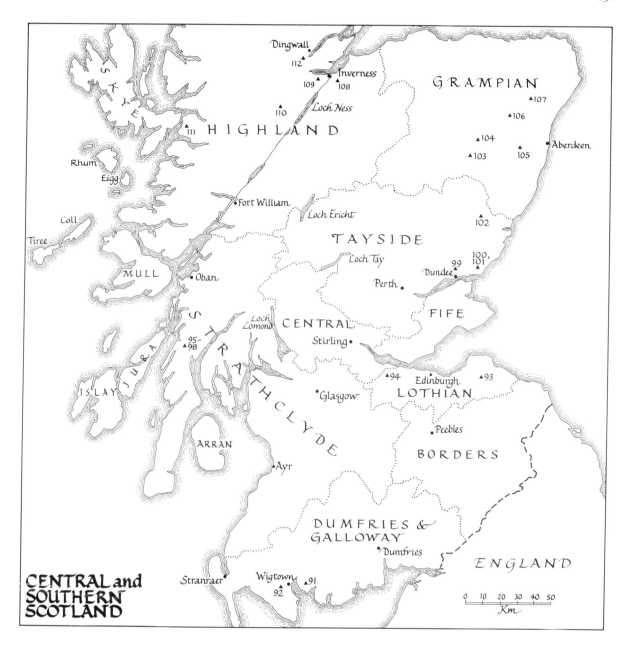

SKYE

Dingwall
▲112
▲109 •Inverness
▲108
GRAMPIAN
▲110 Loch Ness
▲107
▲111 H I G H L A N D
▲106
▲104
Rhum
▲103 ▲105 •Aberdeen
Eigg

Coll
Fort William Loch Ericht
Tiree
T A Y S I D E
Loch Tay
▲102
MULL Loch Tay
•Oban 99▲ 100,
101▲
Dundee
Perth• F I F E
S Loch CENTRAL
T Lomond
R Stirling•
95- A
98 T
▲ H Edinburgh
JURA C ▲94 ▲93
L Y L O T H I A N
ISLAY D •Glasgow
E
•Peebles
ARRAN B O R D E R S

•Ayr

D U M F R I E S &
G A L L O W A Y
•Dumfries E N G L A N D
Stranraer• Wigtown•
▲91
92▲

CENTRAL and
SOUTHERN
SCOTLAND

0 10 20 30 40 50
Km

The façade of Cairnholy I, in its unspoiled setting overlooking Wigtown Bay.
On the right, behind the tall stones, can be seen the slabs forming the burial chamber.

91

Cairnholy chambered cairns, Kirkcudbright (Dumfries and Galloway Region)

The first tomb the visitor sees, known as Cairnholy I, is the more impressive of the two, particularly the upright stones around the forecourt which leads into the burial chamber. The mound behind is about 164 feet (50 metres) long. Pottery found with some cremated human remains in the tomb has been dated to the late Neolithic or Early Bronze Age, but these are some of the final burials. Flint arrowheads and other pottery found show that the tomb was built earlier in the Neolithic period.

Not far away is Cairnholy II, which is also worth seeing although it has less visual impact, especially if you have just visited Cairnholy I. Excavation has shown that this tomb was also in use during the Neolithic and Early Bronze Ages. After the last burials had been placed in them, the entrances to both these tombs were blocked up with stones.

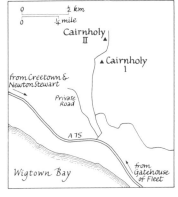

The tallest stone of Cairnholy II rears its head like a Loch Ness monster emerging from the waters.

Map reference:
NX 517538 (metric map 83, 1-inch maps 73 & 80)
Nearest town: Newton Stewart
Nearest village: Creetown
Location: The A75 road between Newton Stewart and Gatehouse of Fleet passes close to the site, and if you are travelling from Gatehouse of Fleet look out for the Auchenlarie Holiday Farm (it is not easy to miss this vast acreage of caravans). Just over a mile (1.6 kilometres) further on, the road bends round to the left, and you should take the minor road off to the right immediately after the bend. Very soon this road bends sharp right, but a lane leads straight ahead, and this should be followed for almost half a mile (.8 kilometre) until the first cairn is reached. Park off the track (which also leads to Cairnholy Farm), and when you have visited Cairnholy I walk up the track for a further 160 yards (150 metres) to Cairnholy II. Both are in the care of the Department of the Environment.

92

Torhouse stone circle,
Wigtown (Dumfries and Galloway Region)

Nineteen smooth boulders form a circle 60 feet (18 metres) in diameter round the edges of a low mound, with a line of three more stones near the centre. This site, which probably dates from the Bronze Age, is in an area rich in cairns and standing stones, and a group of three stones can be seen in a field on the other side of the road.

Map reference:
NX 382565 (metric map 83, 1-inch maps 73 & 80)
Nearest town: Newton Stewart
Nearest village: Wigtown
Location: The circle is by the side of the B733 road 3½ miles (5.5 kilometres) west of Wigtown, and is signposted. It is in the care of the Department of the Environment.

93

**White Castle hillfort,
East Lothian (Lothian Region)**

Yet another beautifully sited Iron Age hillfort, White Castle commands incredible views to the north-west, a vista of valley and plain dominated by the great bulk of Traprain Law. (This hill has remains of a hillfort of great archaeological importance, but sadly it is being steadily quarried away. It is not included in our book, because the remains are visually unimpressive, and because of the relative inaccessibility of the site.)

The three main ramparts of White Castle hillfort are strikingly clear from the road, and they would of course originally have been steeper, but erosion has worn them down. The interior of the fort measures 230 feet (70 metres) by 80 feet (24 metres), and the small hollows show where huts were built. Traces of huts have also been found between the second and innermost of the three ramparts, and these probably represent a post-Roman occupation of the site.

The ramparts of White Castle hillfort are clearly defined in the evening sunlight. The long, dark hump on the horizon is Traprain Law.

Map reference:
NT 613686 (metric map 67, 1-inch map 63)
Nearest town: Haddington
Nearest village: Garvald
Location: The fort lies close beside a lane running across moorland in the Lammermuir Hills south of Haddington. It is 2 miles (3 kilometres) south-east of Garvald, and there is a layby for parking. Free access is always available, by permission of the Lord Abbot and Brethren of Nunraw Abbey.

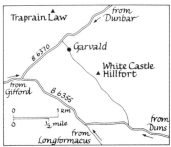

94

Cairnpapple Hill henge and cairn, West Lothian (Lothian Region)

Cairnpapple Hill has a complex history, which falls into five main divisions. Chronologically these are:
1. Seven holes containing cremated human remains date from the late Neolithic period.
2. A henge monument with bank, ditch and twenty-four standing stones was constructed in the Early Bronze Age. Two graves were found within the circle, and one is now protected by a concrete dome which can be entered.
3. Later in the Early Bronze Age a large round cairn was built on the site, partly obtruding into the henge. The stones of the circle were possibly used in building the cairn. The grave which is today preserved was buried beneath the cairn, and two other burials were also found within it. One contained shattered human bones and an unbroken food vessel.
4. The cairn was later enlarged, and two burials dating from this period have been found.
5. At the east of the henge four rock-cut graves were made, intended for bodies placed full-length, but none were found in them. They may possibly date from the early Iron Age.

Careful examination enabled archaeologists to establish the sequence of construction at Cairnpapple Hill, and the site is laid out so that with the aid of the plan provided in the Department of the Environment's leaflet the remains of the different phases can be easily observed.

Map reference:
NS 987717 (metric map 65, 1-inch map 61)
Nearest town: Bathgate
Nearest village: Torphichen
Location: Cairnpapple Hill is beside a minor road in rural countryside 2 miles (3 kilometres) north-east of Bathgate, and can be approached either from there or from Torphichen to the north-west. There is a small layby for parking, and an uphill walk of 200 yards (180 metres) to the site, which is in the care of the Department of the Environment. It is open during standard hours. An entrance fee is payable, and a leaflet is available. A small museum houses the finds.

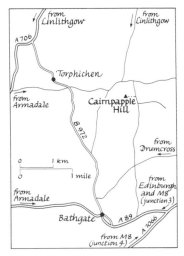

Inside the cairn. A Bronze Age burial and two beakers were found in a pit surrounded by a kerb of stones.

95

Kilmartin linear cairn cemetery, Argyll (Strathclyde Region)

The Kilmartin area of Argyll is a veritable cornucopia of prehistoric sites – cairns, inscribed rocks, stone circles and standing stones especially. Some, however, are not readily accessible, being positioned in the middle of a crop field with no trodden path through the standing corn, or being hidden away in some remote corner and needing skilful map-reading to track down. So here we describe eight of the most accessible sites as at July 1976, when we visited the area. If you have time and persistence, you may be able to locate other sites named in other guidebooks. Two other important relics in the area which are worth visiting, but are not included here because of their later date, are the early Christian crosses and later grave slabs in Kilmartin churchyard; and Dunadd fort, said to have been the capital of Dalriada, the Scottish kingdom, in the Dark Ages.

The five cairns which make up the Kilmartin linear cemetery are, starting in the north, Glebe cairn, Nether Largie north cairn, Nether Largie mid cairn, Nether Largie south cairn, and Ri Cruin cairn.

Glebe cairn All that can be seen now is a huge pile of large pebbles, but when this Early Bronze

Nether Largie north cairn

Ri Cruin cairn. The carved axe heads can just be discerned on the end slab of the cist.

Nether Largie mid cairn

Kilmartin is 8 miles (13 kilometres) north of Lochgilphead and 27 miles (43 kilometres) south of Oban.

Glebe cairn
NR 833989 (metric map 55, 1-inch map 52)
The cairn is in a field behind the church at Kilmartin, and is approached along a footpath which starts beside the petrol station (actually between the petrol station and the sewage works). It is signposted there.

Nether Largie north cairn
NR 831985 (metric map 55, 1-inch map 52)

Nether Largie mid cairn
NR 831984 (metric map 55, 1-inch map 52)
Both the north and mid cairns are reached from the south. Park at the end of the lane which leads north to the cairns but is not suitable for vehicles. The cairns are signposted at this point.

Nether Largie south cairn
NR 828979 (metric map 55, 1-inch map 52)
This cairn is reached from the minor road close by, where it is signposted.

Ri Cruin cairn
NR 826971 (metric map 55, 1-inch map 52)
The cairn is reached from a minor road not far from its junction with the B8025 road. It is signposted, and there is room to park on the grass verge.

All five cairns are in the care of the Department of the Environment.

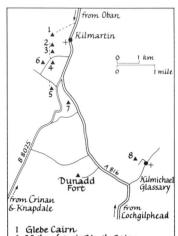

1 Glebe Cairn
2 Nether Largie North Cairn
3 Nether Largie Mid Cairn
4 Nether Largie South Cairn
5 Ri Cruin Cairn
6 Temple Wood Stone Circle (96)
7 Dunchraigaig Cairn (97)
8 Kilmichael Glassary Inscribed Stone (98)

Age cairn was excavated in 1864 two stone cists were found, containing food vessels and a jet bead necklace.

Nether Largie north cairn covers a burial chamber which can be entered from the top. Inside is a stone burial cist whose capstone bears cup marks and carvings of axe heads.

Nether Largie mid cairn Like the north cairn, this dates from the Early Bronze Age. Two stone cists are visible, and originally these would have been covered by pebbles. In fact the cairn was once 10 feet (3 metres) high, but, as with the other cairns in this cemetery, many stones have been carted away over the centuries for road-mending and other purposes.

Nether Largie south cairn This cairn is the oldest of the five, dating from the Neolithic period. In the centre is a four-compartment burial chamber built of large stones which when excavated in 1864 was found to contain cremated burials and pottery. In the edges of the cairn are two stone cists (one visible), probably inserted later in the Early Bronze Age.

Ri Cruin cairn Three stone cists were exposed in this Bronze Age cairn when stones were removed from the body of the cairn. The southern cist has an end slab carved with axe-heads.

Nether Largie south cairn

96

**Temple Wood stone circle,
Argyll (Strathclyde Region)**

Thirteen stones remain out of an original twenty in
this circle of 40-foot (12 metres) diameter, and
spiral carvings can be seen at the base of one of the
northern stones. Inside the circle is a stone burial
cist, and this indicates that the stone circle was
probably a kerb surrounding a large cairn.

Right The cist inside the circle.
Below The stone with spiral carvings at its base.
Bottom right An overall view of the circle.

Map reference:
NR 827978 (metric map 55, 1-inch map 52)
Nearest town: Lochgilphead
Nearest village: Kilmartin
Location: The circle, which is in the care of the
Department of the Environment and is
signposted, is beside a minor road about 200
yards (180 metres) south-west of Nether
Largie south cairn. (See sketch map on page
138.)

97

Dunchraigaig cairn, Argyll (Strathclyde Region)

Three stone cists were found in this Early Bronze Age cairn, and they contained burnt and unburnt bodies, food vessels, a stone axe and a flint knife. The south cist is covered by a large capstone.

Map reference:
NR 833968 (metric map 55, 1-inch map 52)
Nearest town: Lochgilphead
Nearest village: Kilmartin
Location: A short distance to the south-east of the linear cairn cemetery at Kilmartin, Dunchraigaig is close beside the A816 road and in a grove of trees. (See sketch map on page 138.) It is signposted, and is in the care of the Department of the Environment.

98

**Kilmichael Glassary inscribed stone,
Argyll (Strathclyde Region)**

There are a number of rock outcrops bearing
prehistoric carvings in the Kilmartin district, but
not many of them are either accessible or easy to
find. Those at Kilmichael Glassary are both, and
well worth visiting if you find this aspect of
prehistory of interest. We have already outlined
the enigma of ancient rock carvings on page 99;
at Kilmichael Glassary cup and ring marks are well
represented, along with simple cups and also
keyhole shapes.

Map reference:
NR 858935 (metric map 55, 1-inch map 52)
Nearest town: Lochgilphead
Nearest village: Kilmichael Glassary
Location: The village of Kilmichael Glassary is
4 miles (6.5 kilometres) north of Lochgilphead
along the A816 road. In the village, turn left
opposite the church and you will see the
inscribed stone signposted on your right. (See
sketch map on page 138.) The stone is in the
care of the Department of the Environment.

99

**Tealing souterrain,
Angus (Tayside Region)**

Souterrains (also called fogous and earth-houses)
are widespread in Scotland, but also occur
elsewhere in Britain, and we have already
described two in Cornwall (see pages 17 and 22).
Although the Department of the Environment
signposts in Scotland invariably call them earth-
houses, we prefer to use the less definite description
'souterrain', which means simply 'underground'.
'Earth-house' implies that these structures were
used as dwellings, but this is by no means certain.
Other possibilities are cattle sheds, food stores,
hiding places, and ritual sites.

Some of the Scottish souterrains are now
roofless, and that at Tealing is one of these. All that
remains of this Iron Age structure is a long and
curved stone-lined trench. In the passage wall
close to the doorway is a cup and ring marked
stone. This is visible in the photograph, which also
shows the entrance to the passage.

Map reference:
NO 412381 (metric map 54, 1-inch map 50)
Nearest town: Dundee
Nearest village: Balgray
Location: The souterrain lies in fields behind a
farmhouse at Balgray, which is 4½ miles (7
kilometres) north of the centre of Dundee. It is
signposted, and you can drive through the
farmyard as far as a notice telling you to drive
no further. This is close to a sixteenth-century
dovecot, which is worth a second glance,
especially the interior with its row upon row
of stone nesting boxes. Park by the notice and
walk along the track, following the signs
which point the way to the souterrain
(approximately 200 yards/180 metres). Both
souterrain and dovecot are in the care of the
Department of the Environment.

100

Ardestie souterrain, Angus (Tayside Region)

Ardestie souterrain has a number of features not found at Tealing souterrain, though it is similar in appearance, consisting of a sunken stone-lined passageway 80 feet (24 metres) in length and open to the sky. As can be clearly seen in the photograph, a stone drain runs down the centre of the passage, and on the bank beside it are the outlines of huts and a stone 'tank' in which shellfish were possibly kept fresh in water. This layout suggests that the natives lived in the huts and kept their livestock, and possibly other items, in the souterrain. The site has been excavated, and seems to have been occupied in the first three centuries AD, i.e. the Iron Age, with Picts continuing to live in the huts after the souterrain was no longer in use.

Map reference:
NO 502344 (metric map 54, 1-inch map 50)
Nearest town: Dundee
Nearest village: Mains of Ardestie
Location: The souterrain is not far off the main Dundee–Arbroath road, A92, just to the west of the crossroads with the B962 road, and 4½ miles (7 kilometres) north-east of Dundee. Park in the gateway (taking care not to block access to the field), from where it is a walk of 300 yards (270 metres) along the fieldside to the souterrain, which is signposted and is in the care of the Department of the Environment.

Map reference:
NO 511359 (metric map 54, 1-inch map 50)
Nearest town: Dundee
Nearest village: Newbigging
Location: Carlungie souterrain lies approximately 7½ miles (12 kilometres) north-east of Dundee, beside a minor road which runs north-west off the main Dundee–Arbroath road, A92. At this point the souterrain is signposted. Park on the grass verge by the narrow lane and follow the path (100 yards/90 metres) across the field to the souterrain, taking care not to harm whatever crop is being cultivated. (See sketch map on page 143.) The site is in the care of the Department of the Environment.

101

Carlungie souterrain, Angus (Tayside Region)

Carlungie souterrain is the most complex of the three examples in Angus described here, but again it is open to the sky. (For a Scottish example whose roof is intact, see Culsh souterrain, page 149.) The passage is 150 feet (45.5 metres) long, and curves round, with narrower minor passageways leading off it. It must have been a terrifying place to enter when the roof was in position, and it seems hardly possible that people ever built such places to live in.

Even with a constant light source in the form of primitive lamps or a large fire, it would not have been either a comfortable or a convenient place to live. But when this site was excavated, traces of eight huts were found close by, which suggests that Iron Age man used this souterrain for other purposes than a dwelling. Caves have always held a fascination for mankind, and it has been suggested that to enter one symbolised a re-entry into the womb, the protective womb of Mother Earth. It is not impossible that some souterrains were built as artificial caves for religious or magical rituals.

102

The White Caterthun and
Brown Caterthun hillforts, Angus (Tayside Region)

The ruined stone walls encircling the top of the White Caterthun are an impressive feature of this Iron Age hillfort. Two banks with a ditch between them form the outer defences, enclosing an area of about 2 acres (.7 hectares), and inside this are two massive stone walls, which were probably originally 40 feet/12 metres (the inside wall) and 20 feet/6 metres (the outside wall) thick, though rubble from them now spreads much further. Traditionally, the stones were carried here in one morning by a witch in her apron.

Three-quarters of a mile (1.2 kilometres) away on the neighbouring hilltop is the Brown Caterthun hillfort, protected by six lines of fortification. Although there are footpaths to both hillforts, the White Caterthun is both the nearest and the most impressive.

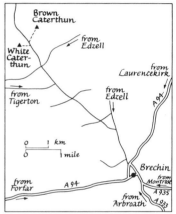

Map references:
White Caterthun
NO 548660 (metric map 44, 1-inch map 50)
Brown Caterthun
NO 555669 (metric map 44, 1-inch map 50)
Nearest town: Brechin
Nearest village: Tigerton
Location: The forts lie either side of a minor road leading north-west from Brechin, and are 5 miles (8 kilometres) from that town. They are signposted, and there is parking space beside the road. The footpath up to the White Caterthun is about 400 yards (360 metres), while that up to the Brown Caterthun is about 800 yards (720 metres). Both hillforts are in the care of the Department of the Environment.

The stone ramparts on top of the White Caterthun.

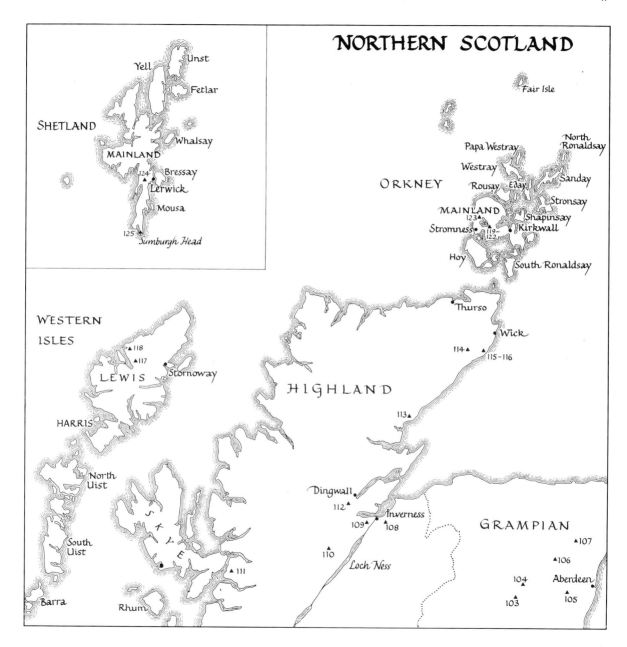

NORTHERN SCOTLAND

SHETLAND

Yell
Unst
Fetlar
Whalsay
MAINLAND
124
Bressay
Lerwick
Mousa
125
Sumburgh Head

Fair Isle

Papa Westray
North Ronaldsay
Westray
ORKNEY
Rousay
Eday
Sanday
Stronsay
MAINLAND
123
Shapinsay
Stromness
119-
Kirkwall
122
Hoy
South Ronaldsay

Thurso
Wick
114
115-116

WESTERN ISLES

118
117
LEWIS
Stornoway

HARRIS

HIGHLAND

113

North Uist

S K Y E

Dingwall
112
Inverness
109
108
GRAMPIAN

110

111

South Uist

Loch Ness

107
106
104
Aberdeen
103
105

Barra

Rhum

103

Tomnaverie recumbent stone circle, Aberdeen (Grampian Region)

The recumbent stone circle is a type of stone circle that is peculiar to the Aberdeen area, its special feature being not, as its name suggests, that all the stones are recumbent, but that a normal circle of standing stones contains within its perimeter one huge stone on its side flanked by two large uprights. The significance of this is not known, nor can it even be guessed at, but the structure resembles a blocked doorway, and this may be a clue to its purpose.

The Tomnaverie circle is unusually sited on a hilltop which has been quarried away right to the edge of the stone circle. The site actually has two rings of stones one inside the other, which results in a rather confused picture, as the photograph demonstrates, but the recumbent stone stands out well enough, being 11 feet (3.3 metres) long. The circle has not been excavated, but probably dates to the Early Bronze Age.

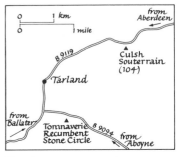

Map reference:
NJ 488035 (metric map 37, 1-inch maps 39 & 42)
Nearest town: Aboyne
Nearest village: Tarland
Location: 4 miles (6.5 kilometres) north-west of Aboyne, the circle lies not far south of the B9094 road to Tarland. It is signposted and there is room to park in the gateway. Follow the track up and round to the left, and you will see the stones, surrounded by a fence, at the top of the hill. They are in the care of the Department of the Environment.

104

Culsh souterrain, Aberdeen (Grampian Region)

This is by far the most exciting of the accessible souterrains in eastern Scotland, because the roof is intact and you can walk into a curved pitch-black passage that extends several yards back into the bank. The photograph above shows the entrance; that on the right gives some idea of the interior.

Map reference:
NJ 505055 (metric map 37, 1-inch maps 39 & 42)
Nearest town: Aboyne
Nearest village: Tarland
Location: 5 miles (8 kilometres) north-west of Aboyne and 1½ miles (2.5 kilometres) north-east of Tarland, this souterrain lies outside Culsh Farm and right beside the B9119 road, where there is room to park. (See sketch map on page 148.) It is signposted, and a torch is available at the farm for those who do not have their own. A light of some kind is essential unless you have nerves of steel and are accustomed to walking forward into velvety blackness! The souterrain is in the care of the Department of the Environment.

105

Cullerlie stone circle,
Aberdeen (Grampian Region)

This Bronze Age circle of eight boulders encloses an area where many small fires had been lit, and eight small cairns had been constructed over pits where corpses had been burnt. This use of the circle as a burial ground very probably followed much later, when the real significance of the stone circle was forgotten or no longer important.

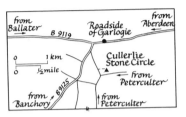

Map reference:
NJ 784042 (metric map 38, 1-inch map 40)
Nearest town: Aberdeen
Nearest village: Roadside of Garlogie
Location: 10 miles (16 kilometres) west of the centre of Aberdeen, this circle lies beside a minor road a short distance to the south of the B9119 Ballater road. It is signposted, and there is a small layby for parking. The circle is in a clearing beyond a small grove of trees, and is in the care of the Department of the Environment.

106

East Aquhorthies recumbent stone circle, Aberdeen (Grampian Region)

This is an attractive example of a recumbent stone circle. Nine upright stones plus a large recumbent one and two flanking stones form a circle of about 63½ feet (19.5 metres) in diameter. We detected some diamond-shaped and some narrower stones, such as are evident at Avebury (see page 58).

Map reference:
NJ 732208 (metric map 38, 1-inch map 40)
Nearest town: Inverurie

Location: The stone circle is 2½ miles (4 kilometres) west of Inverurie, beside a farm track near East Aquhorthies Farm. 1½ miles (2.5 kilometres) west of Inverurie, follow the 'dead-end' road for 1 mile (1.6 kilometres), then take the road to East Aquhorthies Farm. A track on the right leads to the circle, but it has a poor surface so it is wise to park at the end and walk the 100 yards (90 metres) to the circle, which is in the care of the Department of the Environment.

Map reference:
NJ 748289 (metric map 38, 1-inch map 40)
Nearest town: Inverurie
Nearest village: Daviot
Location: Daviot lies 5 miles (8 kilometres) to the north-east of Inverurie, and the circle is ½ mile (.8 kilometres) further north-east, behind a small wood. It is signposted by the lane, and there is room to park in front of the scout hut. A path of 150 yards (135 metres) leads through the wood to the circle, which is in the care of the Department of the Environment.

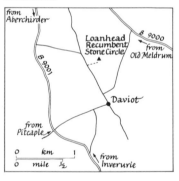

107

**Loanhead recumbent stone circle,
Aberdeen (Grampian Region)**

Here is another example of a stone circle being used for funerary purposes, possibly at a later date. The most notable feature of the site is the huge recumbent stone; but the 1934 excavation revealed other interesting features. The circle of standing stones (66 feet/20.5 metres in diameter) encloses a ring cairn of small boulders and other smaller cairns had been built round the five standing stones lying outside the circle. A cist beneath one of these contained a Middle Bronze Age cup, and pottery from the Late Bronze Age and Iron Age were also discovered. This represents a late use of the circle and ring cairn, which are thought to have been constructed in the Early Bronze Age. A hearth was found in the ring cairn, which may indicate its use as a dwelling at some time, almost certainly when the site had lost its meaning and was seen simply as a convenient place to live.

108

Clava cairns, Inverness (Highland Region)

This most impressive site, not far from the tourist haunt of Culloden battlefield, comprises three large cairns of stones, each surrounded by a circle of shapely standing stones. The circle surrounding the cairn nearest the entrance is 103 feet (31 metres) in diameter, and the cairn can be entered along a passage. Both passage and central burial chamber are now open to the sky, however, as is

the case with all three cairns (though the central cairn has no entrance passage). Bones and pottery were found in the first cairn during the 1828 excavation, the second cairn revealed flint flakes during its 1857 excavation, and the cairn furthest from the entrance contained just a few bones when excavated in 1858. Cup marks can be found on some of the stones.

This site has been examined by Professor Alexander Thom, who discovered that the two entrance passages align exactly, and that the alignment passes through two of the stones

An overall view of the Clava cairns showing the three cairns and some of the standing stones.

surrounding the central non-aligned cairn. The significance of this is that the passage graves were probably constructed in Neolithic times, and the stone circles later, during the Bronze Age. The alignment points to the midwinter sun's setting position, indicating that at some time the site had an astronomical function. The implications in Thom's discoveries at Clava are summed up by Euan Mackie when he comments in his *Scotland: An Archaeological Guide* that 'The Clava group provides a fascinating hint of links between the geometry and astronomy of the stone circles of the early 2nd millennium BC with the Neolithic passage graves of an earlier epoch.'

Looking along the entrance passage of one of the cairns.

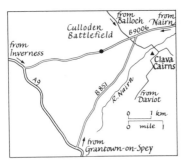

Map reference:
NH 757445 (metric map 27, 1-inch map 28)
Nearest town: Inverness
Location: 6 miles (9.5 kilometres) east of the centre of Inverness and 1 mile (1.6 kilometres) east-south-east of Culloden battlefield, the cairns lie close beside a minor road off the B851 road. There is a very small parking space beside the lane, and the cairns, in a clearing surrounded by trees, are in the care of the Department of the Environment.

109

**Craig Phadrig vitrified fort,
Inverness (Highland Region)**

Vitrified forts are found chiefly in eastern Scotland, and the circumstances in which the unusual phenomenon of vitrification occurred still remain controversial. The defences of the earliest Scottish forts were built of timber inside rubble walls, and the theory supported by many archaeologists is that when the forts were attacked and set on fire in windy weather, the great heat generated in the burning wood would be sufficient to fuse the stone walls into a slaggy mass. An alternative suggestion is that the fort-builders themselves used this method to consolidate the walls and thus make stronger defences. We do not know if any experiments have been carried out to see if either of these theories is feasible; but in view of the large number of vitrified forts neither explanation sounds entirely convincing. However, they are certainly preferable to the suggestion advocated by supporters of the 'ancient astronauts' theory, that the forts were attacked from the air by interplanetary spacemen using ray guns!

Craig Phadrig is one of the more accessible vitrified forts. As a hillfort it would not be worth a visit by the layman, were it not for the exposed vitrified rock. Being on a hilltop in the middle of a forest, it is not easy to make out its layout, but there are two lines of ramparts, both vitrified, enclosing a flat rectangular area measuring 98 feet (30 metres) by 262 feet (80 metres). The inner rampart stands 13 feet (4 metres) high externally. During excavations in the early 1970s, radiocarbon dating revealed that the ramparts were probably built around 500 BC. The Forestry Commission reference to a 'Pictish fort' on their noticeboard by the car park relates to a later occupation of the site.

The fort is thought to have been the dwelling-place of the Pictish king Brude, and the story goes that in the sixth century AD, when St Columba was in Scotland to convert the natives to Christianity, he climbed up to the fort to see King Brude, but the gates were barred against him. According to

Adamnan, the saint's biographer, Columba 'traced the sign of the Lord's Cross on them and, knocking, laid his hands against the doors and immediately the bolts are violently thrust back and the doors open in haste of their own account and, their being thus opened, the Saint thereupon enters with his companions'. This miracle caused Brude to be baptised and to give his permission for the conversion of his people. Thus Craig Phadrig became the first Christian foundation in the highlands.

The hillfort is one feature along a Forestry Commission forest trail, and in good weather the walk through the conifers and the steep climb uphill to the fort are well rewarded by magnificent views as well as an opportunity to examine vitrified rock closely. The Forestry Commission have erected an information board at the start of the walk, which identifies the trees to be seen. In the forest are the twelve species of conifers planted on a commercial scale throughout Britain.

The outer ramparts

Map reference:
NH 640453 (metric map 26, 1-inch map 28)
Nearest town: Inverness
Nearest village: Leachkin
Location: The fort is only 1½ miles (2.5 kilometres) to the west of the centre of Inverness, and is approached along minor roads south of the A9 road. Leave this road where the Caledonian Canal crosses it, and follow the minor road towards Leachkin. A lane leads uphill beside the fort, and just before the trees begin on your right is a signboard (partly concealed) reading 'Forestry Commission Craig Phadrig Forest, car park, forest walk and Pictish fort'. Park in the car park and follow the clearly marked path of approximately 500 yards (450 metres) up to the fort.

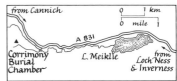

Map reference:
NH 383303 (metric map 26, 1-inch map 27)
Nearest town: Inverness
Nearest village: Cannich
Location: The cairn is in Glen Urquhart, close
beside a minor road which leaves the A831
road 23 miles (37 kilometres) south-west of
Inverness. It is signposted at this point, so it is
not too difficult to find. The lane is narrow
and twisting, so take care – we almost
collided head-on with a speeding van during
our visit! The lane is, however, wider near the
cairn, so there is room to park in safety. The
site is in the care of the Department of the
Environment.

110

**Corrimony chambered cairn,
Inverness (Highland Region)**

This Neolithic chambered cairn is similar to those
at Clava (page 153), and the visible remains are a
heap of large pebbles surrounding a central burial
chamber of stone with a stone-lined passageway
leading to it. It is possible to enter the chamber
along the passage, though the roof is low and some
agility is needed. The chamber is now open to the
sky, so it is also possible to climb up the side of the
cairn and view it from above. Notice a large cup-
marked stone lying on top of the mound if you do
climb on to it. Also as at Clava, the cairn is
surrounded by a stone circle, with eleven stones in
this case. The cairn was excavated in 1952 and
traces of a crouched burial were found inside the
burial chamber.

111

Dun Telve and Dun Troddan brochs, Inverness (Highland Region)

The broch is a unique structure found only in Scotland, and Euan MacKie's summary of its significance is worth repeating here. In an article entitled 'The Brochs of Scotland',* he tells us that 'Apart from Stonehenge they appear to be the only really advanced architectural creation of prehistoric and early historic times which was invented entirely within Britain, instead of being imported here from elsewhere. Nearly every other major class of stone building from Neolithic times onwards – chambered cairns, hill-forts, Roman forts and buildings, early stone castles and Romanesque and Gothic cathedrals - was developed first on the continent of Europe and then introduced to the British Isles. Yet no structures remotely similar to a broch are known outside Scotland so it seems that this building - which may fairly be claimed as Man's greatest architectural achievement in drystone masonry - was developed wholly in Scotland.'

Brochs are generally considered to date from the Iron Age, and they were probably defensive dwellings or refuges. There are over 500 in the 'Atlantic province' of Scotland, and one of the best preserved examples is Dun Carloway broch (see page 164). Basically, brochs were round, towerlike buildings, with a shape somewhat similar to today's cooling towers at a generating station. The walls were double and the space between the two was the living area and carried a spiral staircase linking each floor with that above and below. The inner circular courtyard was probably open to the sky and could have housed the livestock. Most impressive is the fact that the whole construction was of dry stone (i.e. no mortar was used, each stone being held in place by the weight of those above). With its single entrance closed and well defended, the broch was probably a secure haven for those inside.

*In *Recent Work in Rural Archaeology*, edited by P. J. Fowler (Moonraker Press 1975).

Dun Telve (below) and Dun Troddan (above) are two well-preserved brochs which stand only ¼ mile (.4 kilometre) apart, near Glenelg. They are 33 feet (10 metres) and 25 feet (7.6 metres) high respectively. The stones for both brochs were said to have come from a quarry further along the glen, and to have been passed along a line of men.

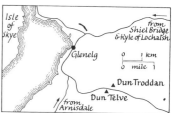

Map references:
Dun Telve
NG 829172 (metric map 33, 1-inch map 35)
Dun Troddan
NG 834172 (metric map 33, 1-inch map 35)
Nearest town: Kyle of Lochalsh
Nearest village: Glenelg
Location: The brochs are in one of the wilder and less accessible parts of Scotland, close to the west coast, but luckily a minor road passes very close to them. 6 miles (9.5 kilometres) from Kyle of Lochalsh as the crow flies, but nearer 30 miles (48 kilometres) by road, they are south-east of Glenelg, along a minor road which eventually peters out in the mountains. Both are in the care of the Department of the Environment.

112

**Knockfarrel vitrified fort,
Ross and Cromarty (Highland Region)**

Fine examples of vitrification can be seen around the plateau on top of Knockfarrel hill, where the hillfort covered a rectangular area 124 feet (38 metres) by 426 feet (130 metres). The usual explanation that is applied to all similar examples of vitrification also applies here – burning of the timber and rubble ramparts during an attack – and if this is the true explanation, the destruction of these forts must have been terrible to witness.

Giants were said to live on Knockfarrel and two stories are told about them, one involving fire. The giants were hunting on Skye when they saw flames and, fearing for the safety of their families, hastened home just in time to rescue their wives who had been shut in a hut which was then set on fire by their enemies. The other tale is about a stone-throwing competition between a giant and a dwarf. The giant threw a stone carved with an eagle over to Fodderty, whereupon the dwarf picked up the two huge stone gateposts of the fort and hurled them after the eagle stone.

Knockfarrel is a fine vantage point, in the hills between Strathpeffer and Loch Ussie, and the walk to the top with only sheep, rabbits and curlews for company is strongly recommended.

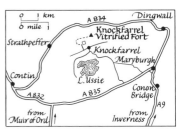

Map reference:
NH 505585 (metric map 26, 1-inch map 27)
Nearest town: Dingwall
Nearest village: Knockfarrel
Location: The fort is well off the beaten track, and several miles of driving along narrow but well-surfaced lanes is necessary to reach it, although the site is only 2½ miles (4 kilometres) west of Dingwall as the crow flies. Leaving the main A9 road at Maryburgh south of Dingwall and following the route shown on the sketch map will bring you to a lane which ends beside a white bungalow. Park here, taking care not to block their exit, and cross the stile where the road ends. Follow the track round and along the ridge to the top of the hill.

Looking along the hillfort. Some of the vitrified stone can be seen in the foreground.

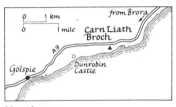

Map reference:
NC 871013 (metric map 17, 1-inch maps 15 & 22)
Nearest town: Brora
Nearest village: Golspie
Location: The broch is close beside the A9 road 2 miles (3 kilometres) north-east of Golspie and 3 miles (5 kilometres) south-west of Brora, and it lies between the road and the sea. When the road goes on to a raised embankment (1 mile/1.6 kilometres east of the entrance to Dunrobin Castle), park on the large layby to the left (if you are approaching from Golspie). Cross the road, climb over the fence and down the bank, and the broch is ahead of you on a mound.

113

Carn Liath broch,
Sutherland (Highland Region)

There are many brochs marked on the Ordnance Survey maps of northern Scotland, but most are scarcely worth visiting. All that remains is a grass-grown mound or heap of rubble. Carn Liath, although not as good as the best, is worth visiting, for the walls still stand 12 feet (3.6 metres) high in places and the entrance passage and lintelled doorway are well preserved. The remains of buildings outside the broch indicate a later use when a fortified dwelling was no longer necessary.

Map reference:
ND 188418 (metric maps 11 & 12, 1-inch maps
11 & 16)
Nearest town: Wick
Nearest village: Latheron
Location: The stones are close by a minor road
which leaves the A895 road at Achavanich,
approximately 12 miles (19 kilometres)
south-west of Wick. Park by the roadside and
go through the gate to the stones, which are
on lonely, open moorland.

114

Loch Stemster standing stones, Caithness (Highland Region)

The moors of Caithness, littered with ruined crofts, farms, cottages and houses, and rich in flora and fauna which you hardly notice if you simply rush along the A9 in your car, are a good hunting ground for prehistoric sites. A particularly impressive and unusual site is the U-shaped arrangement of thirty-six standing stones to the south of Loch Stemster. During the several thousand years since they were erected, the thin slabs of stone have become overgrown with lichens in many subtle shades. There can be little doubt that the men who erected these stones were well aware of their aesthetic qualities, but did they have any other purpose? Euan MacKie tells us in *Scotland: An Archaeological Guide* that some of the stones seem to indicate Mount Morven to the south, and that the setting may be an astronomical foresight. The photograph shows one arm of the U; the stones continue round to the left.

115

The Grey Cairns of Camster, Caithness (Highland Region)

The Grey Cairns of Camster are two restored Neolithic chambered cairns, one round and the other long. Camster round cairn has a diameter of 59 feet (18 metres), and the internal burial chamber can be reached along a low, narrow passage. You do not need a torch, because the chamber roof has had a skylight let into it, but it is a thrilling experience to enter the cairn nevertheless – especially for those who know the sensation of claustrophobia. The passage, 20 feet (6.1 metres) long, is only $2\frac{1}{2}$–$3\frac{1}{2}$ feet (.7–1.1 metres) high, which means that it has to be negotiated on hands and knees. At the inner end of the passage is an antechamber, but unless you have a torch it will be no more than an area of blackness on either side of you. The burial chamber is well lit and can be seen to be a tall, circular, corbelled room 10 feet (3 metres) high. Charcoal, ashes, burnt and unburnt bones and broken pots were discovered in the 1865 excavations, plus two skeletons which had been placed in the passage before it was blocked with stones.

A short distance away is Camster long cairn, which at the time of writing (mid 1976) is being excavated and restored. It is an unusual structure with external steps, and contains two burial chambers. These seem to have been within separate round cairns originally, which were later enclosed in one long cairn.

Map reference:
ND 260442 (metric maps 11 & 12, 1-inch maps 11 & 16)
Nearest town: Wick
Nearest village: Lybster
Location: The cairns are close to a north–south minor road which leaves the A9 road east of Lybster. They are 5 miles (8 kilometres) north of the junction with the main road, and are signposted along the lane. Park by the roadside and walk across the duckboards to the round cairn, then to the long cairn which is a few yards further north. Both are in the care of the Department of the Environment.

Camster round cairn

116

**The Hill o' Many Stanes,
Caithness (Highland Region)**

This unusual site is well described as the 'Hill o'
Many Stanes': around 200 small stones are
arranged in twenty-two apparently parallel rows.
'Apparently parallel' because surveys have shown
that in fact the formation is slightly fan-shaped.
Why would anyone go to the trouble of erecting
stones in this pattern? Professor Alexander Thom
thinks the site may have had an astronomical

function, and that the stones could have formed a
kind of grid or computer by means of which
observations of the moon were plotted. These ideas
are given in more detail in his books *Megalithic
Sites in Britain* (where the site is referred to as 'Mid
Clyth') and *Megalithic Lunar Observatories*. So
although the Hill o' Many Stanes is not a dramatic
site to visit, the discovery that it was a lunar
observatory some 4,000 or more years ago makes it
a place where one can pause to wonder at the
knowledge and skill possessed by our distant
ancestors. Have we really progressed all that far
since 2000 BC?

Map reference:
ND 295384 (metric map 11, 1-inch maps 11 &
16)
Nearest town: Wick
Nearest village: Lybster
Location: The stone rows lie close to a minor
road which leaves the A9 road 4 miles (6.5
kilometres) north-east of Lybster. The site is
signposted at this point, so is not difficult to
find. It is less than ½ mile (.8 kilometre) along
the lane; park by the roadside and walk
through the gate on to the hill slope. The site
is in the care of the Department of the
Environment. (See sketch map on page 161.)

117

Callanish standing stones, Lewis (Western Isles)

Some of the oldest rocks to be found on the surface of the earth are in Scotland, and in this strange, age-old landscape on the west coast of the island of Lewis is the remarkable site of Callanish, regarded by some as second in importance only to Stonehenge. This is a complex site and, probably due to its remoteness, not a great deal is known about it. The principal feature is a circle of tall stone slabs. Leading from this in a northerly direction is an avenue of two rows of stones, while

The Callanish stones resemble figures, and are sometimes known as Fir Bhreig (false men).
In the middle of the last century, peat 5 feet (1.5 metres) deep was removed from around the stones.

to the east, south and west run shorter single rows, thus making the whole layout a basic cross shape. The circle is formed by thirteen stones and has a radius of 21 feet (6.5 metres), with a single stone 15 feet (4.6 metres) tall standing near the centre. Also inside the circle are the remains of a chambered round cairn of Neolithic type, but archaeologists are undecided whether this was built before or after the stone circle and stone rows, which have all been dated to the Bronze Age. The northern avenue has nineteen stones still standing and is 275 feet (8.3 metres) long and 27 feet (8 metres) wide; the other three rows have four, four and six (in the southern row) stones. In 1857 the site was excavated, but only a fragment of human bone was found, so it is probable that the grave was emptied in ancient times.

As with Stonehenge, recent research has been directed to accurately surveying the layout of the site and the alignments that some of the stones make with points on the horizon at which the sun, moon and some major stars are seen to rise or set at certain times in the year. For example, Professor Alexander Thom, who has surveyed hundreds of circles throughout the British Isles, finds that

looking south along the line of the stone avenue gives the point at which the midsummer full moon sets behind Mount Clisham, 16 miles (26 kilometres) distant. And the other stone rows also indicate significant points on the horizon.

Local tradition explains the presence of these stones by saying that when the giants of old who then lived on the island refused to be christened or to build a church, St Kieran, who led the Christian mission to the island, turned them to stone. Another story tells how in a time of famine a white cow appeared from the sea and directed the women to take their milk pails to the old stone circle, where she provided everyone with one pailful of milk each night. A witch tried to get two pailsful but without success, so she returned next time with a sieve with which she milked the cow dry. After that it was never again seen at the Callanish stones. Another local belief of this Gaelic-speaking community was that when the sun rose on midsummer morn the 'shining one' walked along the stone avenue, his arrival heralded by the cuckoo's call. Could this be a much-distorted memory of the astronomical significance of the Callanish stones?

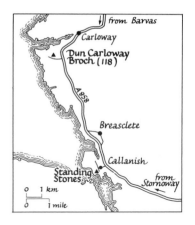

Map reference:
NB 214331 (metric maps 8 & 13, 1-inch maps 8 & 12)
Nearest town: Stornoway
Nearest village: Callanish
Location: 13 miles (21 kilometres) due west of Stornoway, the Callanish stones are at the southern end of Callanish village, and the site, in the care of the Department of the Environment, is well signposted. A leaflet is available.

118

Dun Carloway broch, Lewis (Western Isles)

Dun Carloway is one of the best preserved brochs, the tallest part still standing some 22 feet (6.7 metres) high. The overall diameter is 47 feet (14.3 metres) and the inner courtyard is 24 feet (7.5 metres) across. Originally the walls might have been about 43 feet (13 metres) high. The double wall typical of brochs is well preserved, showing how tiers of galleries were linked by a stone staircase within the hollow wall.

Map reference:
NB 190413 (metric maps 8 & 13, 1-inch maps 8 & 12)
Nearest town: Stornoway
Nearest village: Carloway
Location: 15 miles (24 kilometres) north-west of Stornoway, 5½ miles (9 kilometres) north of Callanish, and 1¼ miles (2 kilometres) south-west of Carloway, the broch stands close to a minor road west of the A858 road, about ¼ mile (.5 kilometre) from the junction with the main road. (See sketch map above.) It is in the care of the Department of the Environment.

119

Maes Howe passage grave, Orkney

'A long time ago was a great treasure hidden here. Lucky will be he who can find the great fortune.

Hákon single-handed bore treasure from this howe.' So reads part of one of the runic inscriptions carved on the stones inside Maes Howe, probably in the twelfth century AD when the Vikings broke into the tomb. They also left pictorial carvings – a dragon, a walrus and a serpent knot – but they

Maes Howe passage grave is one of the finest examples of prehistoric architecture and workmanship in north-west Europe. This photograph is taken inside the tomb, looking back along the entrance passage.

took away all the treasure, and we shall never know what it comprised.

Maes Howe had already been in existence for over 3,500 years when the Vikings raided it, for it is thought to have been constructed around 2500 BC. The skill demonstrated in the stonework shows that the men who built Maes Howe were no savages, but true craftsmen. No mortar was used, and some of the slabs still fit so well together that a knife blade cannot be inserted between them. The tomb is covered by a large mound about 24 feet (7.3 metres) high and 115 feet (35 metres) in diameter, and a long passage (36 feet/11 metres) leads to a tall chamber 15 feet (4.6 metres) square, deep in the mound. In one wall is the doorway (see photograph on page 165), but each of the other three walls contains a square hole nearly 3 feet (1 metre) above the ground. These open out into small chambers which once may have contained burials, and in front of each opening the large stone which was used to block it still stands on the floor (see photograph below).

Map reference:
HY 318127 (metric map 6, 1-inch map 6)
Nearest town: Stromness
Nearest village: Finstown
Location: Maes Howe is on Orkney mainland, just to the north of the main A965 road between Stromness and Kirkwall, and is about 5 miles (8 kilometres) from the former. It is in the care of the Department of the Environment and is open during their standard hours, the key being obtained from the nearby farmhouse, and an admission fee is payable. A leaflet is available.

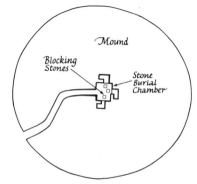

120

Onston chambered cairn, Orkney

Although a concrete dome now covers this tomb, the interior of Onston (sometimes spelt Unstan) cairn has been well preserved, and can be reached along a narrow passage 14 feet (4.3 metres) long which enters the burial chamber at one end. The chamber, 21 feet (6.6 metres) long and 6½ feet (2 metres) wide, is divided on both sides into five compartments or 'stalls' by upright flagstones. Tombs of this design, called 'stalled cairns', are found only in Orkney and Caithness. This one probably dates from around 3000 BC.

When the cairn was excavated in 1884, some interesting finds were made. Human and animal bones were found, together with burnt bones and charcoal, flint arrowheads and pottery fragments. Also during this excavation, two burials were discovered in a small cell which opens off the side wall of the main chamber.

Below left The flagstones dividing the tomb into stalls can be clearly seen. Below Neolithic pottery and flint arrowheads found in the cairn.

Map reference:
HY 283117 (metric map 6, 1-inch map 6)
Nearest town: Stromness
Location: The cairn is beside the Loch of Stenness on Orkney mainland, and a farm road leads to it from the main A965 Stromness–Kirkwall road. It is only 2 miles (3 kilometres) east of Stromness, and is in the care of the Department of the Environment. (See sketch map on page 166.) A full description appears in the Department of the Environment guidebook *Ancient Monuments in Orkney.*

121

**The Stones of Stenness henge
and standing stones, Orkney**

The outer bank and ditch of this henge monument
can now hardly be seen: all that remains are four
standing stones once part of the inner stone circle.
The tallest is about 16 feet (5 metres) high, but not
far away, at the southern end of the Bridge of
Brodgar, is an even taller stone 18½ feet (5.6
metres) high and known as the Watch Stone. This
may have been part of a line of standing stones
linking the Stones of Stenness with the nearby
Ring of Brodgar (see page 169).

Do not be misled by the 'dolmen' which stands
inside this henge. It dates only from AD 1906, when
some fallen stones were 'restored' to what was

then mistakenly thought to have been their
original formation.

According to an eighteenth-century antiquary,
Dr Robert Henry, this site was once known as the
Temple of the Moon, and the Ring of Brodgar as the
Temple of the Sun. Each New Year's Day, the local
people met at Stenness church and danced and
feasted for several days. If a man and woman fell in
love, they went first to the Temple of the Moon,
'where the woman, in presence of the man, fell
down on her knees and prayed to the god Wodden
. . . that he would enable her to perform all the
promises and obligations she had [made]. . . to the
young man present, after which they both went to
the Temple of the Sun, where the man prayed in
like manner before the woman.' Finally they
clasped hands through the hole in the Stone of
Odin (now destroyed) and swore fidelity.

Map reference:
HY 307125 (metric map 6, 1-inch map 6)
Nearest town: Stromness
Location: The Stones of Stenness are on
Orkney mainland, to the east of the B9055
road, ½ mile (.8 kilometre) north of its junction
with the A965 Stromness–Kirkwall road. (See
sketch map on page 166.) The site is in the
care of the Department of the Environment,
and is described in the Department's
guidebook *Ancient Monuments in Orkney.*

122

The Ring of Brodgar henge and stone circle, Orkney

Twenty-seven stones remain out of an original sixty in this impressive stone circle, which is also known as the Ring of Brogar or Broigar. The stones are part of a henge monument, and the surrounding ditch and bank can still be made out, with entrances on the north-west and south-east. The circle had a diameter of about 120 yards (109.7 metres) and the tallest stone today measures 15 feet (4.6 metres). There are carvings on four of the stones, and in a clockwise direction from the north-west entrance they are on stones numbers 3 (a runic inscription), 4 (a cross), 8 (an anvil) and 9 (an ogham inscription). These were carved many years after the erection of the stones, and a tentative dating for this site is the Early Bronze Age. It may have links with similar sites in England, for example Avebury, which is certainly more complex but also possesses the same basic structure of outer bank and ditch and inner stone circle, together with an avenue of stones, the Kennet Avenue, comparable to the line of stones which once may have linked the Ring of Brodgar with the nearby Stones of Stenness.

Map reference:
HY 294134 (metric map 6, 1-inch map 6)
Nearest town: Stromness
Location: The Ring of Brodgar is on Orkney mainland, to the west of the B9055 road, 1½ miles (2.4 kilometres) north of its junction with the A965 Stromness–Kirkwall road. (See sketch map on page 166.) It is in the care of the Department of the Environment, and is described in their guidebook *Ancient Monuments in Orkney.*

Map reference:
HY 231188 (metric map 6, 1-inch map 6)
Nearest town: Stromness
Nearest village: Dounby
Location: Skara Brae is on Orkney mainland, 7 miles (11.3 kilometres) north of Stromness and on the southern side of the Bay of Skaill. It is reached by a footpath round the edge of the bay, a walk of 700 yards (640 metres) from the B9056 road. It is in the care of the Department of the Environment and is open during their standard hours; an admission fee is payable. A detailed guidebook is available, and Skara Brae is also described in the Department of the Environment guidebook *Ancient Monuments in Orkney.*

123

Skara Brae settlement, Orkney

Everyone knows that in AD 79 the Italian city of Pompeii was buried beneath a massive overflow of lava from Mount Vesuvius, and that the long-term result of the disaster was to preserve many unique features of the civilisation of the time. It is not so well known, however, that a natural disaster in the Orkney islands about 3,000 years ago had a similar result. On that occasion a violent storm blew sand over a coastal settlement, causing the inhabitants to leave in haste, and their huts and possessions remained buried beneath the sand until 1850 when another storm stripped away the covering turf and revealed the ruins. Now the site has been carefully excavated and the life-style of its occupants reconstructed from the many artefacts which have been discovered there.

The settlement was well preserved because stone rather than wood (which was probably in short supply) was used for the furniture as well as the building of the actual huts. In the best preserved huts, a hearth can be seen on the floor – the smoke from the fire would have escaped through a hole in the centre of the roof. Opposite the hearth is an upright stone structure with compartments, possibly a 'dresser' used for storage purposes. On either side of the hearth are stone structures identified as beds. These probably contained mattresses of heather, and finds of beads and bones suggest that personal treasures were concealed there, the bones being the remnants of a meal left behind when the storm arose. The edges of the beds were used as fireside seats where the occupants sat and worked, and tools and half-finished items have been found between bed and

Above *An overall view of Skara Brae showing huts and streets, and the coastal position of the site.*
Right *Looking through the entrance into Hut 7. The central hearth and upright stone 'dresser' can be clearly seen.*

hearth. Recesses in the walls may have acted as cupboards, and small 'tanks' let into the ground and lined with clay are thought to have been filled with sea water and used to keep shellfish fresh. Among the everyday objects discovered are pottery, cooking pots containing animal bones, whalebone and stone dishes (some containing red, yellow and blue pigments, which suggest the people may have painted their bodies), stone basins or mortars, stone axe heads, bone adzes, a shovel made from an ox's shoulder-blade, and beads and pendants made from sheep bones, the teeth of cattle and whales, and walrus ivory. (Some of these finds are on display at the site.) The indications are that the villagers kept cattle and sheep, for the bones of these animals are much in evidence. Shellfish too were eaten, but whether they grew crops of any kind is not known. Their clothes were probably made from animal skins; no evidence of cloth-making has been found.

The seven huts to be seen today are small, from 21 by 20 feet (6.4 by 6.1 metres) to 14 by 13 feet (4.3 by 4 metres) in size, and were entered through low (3 feet 9 inches/1.1 metres) and narrow (1 foot 10 inches/.6 metre) doorways cut through the thick walls (4 feet/1.2 metres on average). The huts are linked by covered stone alleyways and the whole settlement was surrounded and almost covered by a huge clayey refuse heap containing ash, bones, shells, dung and sand. This served to protect the village against the inclement weather, and may have been purposely built up rather than having accumulated gradually over the centuries. It is not possible to tell how long the site was occupied, but the remains of earlier settlements have been discovered on the site, and the village visible now is probably Skara Brae 3. Also, the fact that no metal objects have been found dates the occupations to the Neolithic period.

Euan MacKie suggests, in *Science and Society in Prehistoric Britain*, that Skara Brae was no peasant village but a 'palatial structure' housing wise men engaged in astronomical and magical work, and the evidence presented in his book is very persuasive.

124

Clickhimin settlement and broch, Shetland

Clickhimin has a complex history. Remains of fortifications from several periods can be seen, but the earliest occupation would appear to be a farmhouse of the Late Bronze Age (700–500 BC). The house was built round a central hearth, and its remains can still be seen to the north-west of the broch. In the early Iron Age a stone wall was built to fortify the site, with a three-storey blockhouse inside it (only the lower part now remains). In the late Iron Age, serious permanent flooding necessitated emergency rebuilding to keep out the water. Later, a strong stone broch 65 feet (19.8 metres) in diameter and probably 40–50 feet (12–15 metres) high was built, and it still stands over 17 feet (5 metres) high. Brochs were apparently built as fortresses to protect the inhabitants from raiders, and when life became more peaceful they were abandoned. At Clickhimin, when this time came, some demolition took place and a large wheel-house was built inside the broch, similar in design to the smaller ones at Jarlshof (see page 174). This was probably built during the second century AD, and its walls can

still be seen inside the broch. During occupation, refuse was thrown outside, and by investigating the rubbish heap which gradually built up, archaeologists have been able to discover much about the people and their way of life. Pottery and implements of bone and stone including spindle-whorls, together with rings, brooches and beads, were among the items found.

The wheel-house may have been occupied until the ninth century. Flooding at the site, already referred to, caused Clickhimin to be separated from the mainland and a causeway and landing stage were built. Euan MacKie believes that the flooding took place in the later years of Clickhimin's life, probably while the wheel-house was occupied, rather than at the time before the broch was built. (For further details, see his *Scotland: An Archaeological Guide*, pages 275–80.)

One last feature of Clickhimin, which suggests it was once a place of some importance, is a stone which can today be seen on the causeway outside the walls of the fort. This stone bears two carved footprints; in olden times it was customary for new kings to stand barefoot on such footprinted stones during their inauguration ceremonies. This stone was probably moved from its original position when its significance had been forgotten.

Map reference:
HU 464408 (metric map 4, 1-inch maps 3 & 4)
Nearest town: Lerwick
Location: Clickhimin is on Shetland mainland, just west of Lerwick, on a promontory at the southern end of the Loch of Clickhimin and north of the A970 road. It is in the care of the Department of the Environment, and open at 'all reasonable times'. A detailed guidebook entitled *The Brochs of Mousa and Clickhimin* gives a full history of the site and explains what can be seen there.

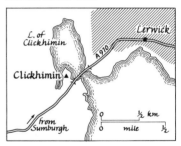

The wall of the broch still stands over 17 feet (5 metres) high. The entrance can be seen on the left, while in the centre foreground is a square stone hearth.

125

Jarlshof settlement, Shetland

At Jarlshof as at Skara Brae in Orkney (see page 170), the site has been preserved by windblown sand, but at Jarlshof the sand accumulated gradually. The history of Jarlshof is rather more complex than that of Skara Brae, in that eight occupation phases have been brought to light:

1. The earliest settlers came here in the second millennium BC. The remains of only one hut have

The location of Jarlshof by the West Voe of Sumburgh is shown here; Sumburgh Head is in the distance. Half the site was eroded away by the sea, and it was this plus the action of violent storms at the end of the last century which brought the remains to sight.

On the right is an aisled round house of the Iron Age; the stone-lined hearth can be seen projecting into the unpaved area. In the centre and on the left are two wheel-houses, and the radial dividing walls (10 feet/3 metres high) of that on the left can be clearly seen. In the background are the remains of the Viking settlement.

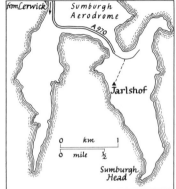

been found, but it is clear that the occupants kept sheep and oxen and ate plenty of shellfish.

2. Six dwellings from the Late Bronze Age settlement have been discovered; their occupants kept sheep and cattle and grew grain, as well as catching fish, seals, wildfowl and shellfish. They used stone, bone and clay for their equipment, and some metal.

3. During the early Iron Age circular stone huts were built. Close by were souterrains probably used for food storage.

4. Later in the Iron Age, possibly around the end of the last century BC and the beginning of the first century AD, a broch was built, and several large oval houses. The way of life of the people seems to have been much the same as it was in the Late Bronze Age, and although some iron was used, the traditional materials were preferred.

5. In the second and third centuries AD, 'wheel-houses' were built. These were circular and divided internally into compartments radiating out from the centre.

6. Viking settlers came to Jarlshof in the early ninth century and built farmsteads where they lived in peace.

7. A medieval farmstead was built at the end of the thirteenth century and this was superseded in the late sixteenth century by

8. The 'New Hall', a stone house occupied by a laird. Sir Walter Scott included this house in his novel *The Pirate*, and it was he who named it Jarlshof.

Remains of all these settlements can still be seen, and the visitor who wishes to follow the development of Jarlshof in more detail is advised to buy the 36-page Department of the Environment guidebook which gives far more information than is possible here.

Map reference:
HU 399095 (metric map 4, 1-inch map 4)
Nearest town: Lerwick
Nearest village: Sumburgh
Location: Situated on the southern tip of Shetland mainland, Jarlshof is 22 miles (35 kilometres) south of Lerwick. It is not far south-east of Sumburgh aerodrome, and is signposted from the nearest road, the A970. It is in the care of the Department of the Environment, open during their standard hours, and an admission fee is payable. There is also a small museum at the site, and a guidebook is available.

126

Other sites on Orkney and Shetland

Orkney and Shetland are rich in impressive prehistoric remains, and those described fully in the previous pages are the most accessible. The adventurous visitor may wish to explore further afield while he is in the area, and the following is a list of more remote places which are also well worth seeing. Fuller descriptions can be found in the Department of the Environment guidebook *Ancient Monuments in Orkney, Scotland: An Archaeological Guide* and *Orkney and Shetland: An Archaeological Guide*. The last also describes other sites which are even more inaccessible, and a visit to any of these more remote sites is advisable only if you have an Ordnance Survey map and compass and know how to use them!

ORKNEY

Cuween Hill chambered cairn HY 364128 (metric map 6, 1-inch map 6) On the mainland. This tomb is entered down a passage 18 feet (5.3 metres) long but less than 3 feet (.9 metres) high.

Grain souterrain HY 442117 (metric map 6, 1-inch map 6) Near Kirkwall on the mainland. An accessible (just! – the passage is 26 feet/7.9 metres long and 3 feet/.9 metre high) underground passage and chamber.

Broch of Gurness, Aikerness HY 383268 (metric map 6, 1-inch map 6) On the coast of the mainland. The tower stands about 10 feet (3 metres) high.

Rennibister souterrain HY 397127 (metric map 6,

The broch of Mousa

1-inch map 6) In a farmyard on the mainland. An accessible underground passage and chamber.

Wideford Hill chambered cairn HY 409122 (metric map 6, 1-inch map 6) A mainland cairn with accessible burial chamber, though the entrance passage is only 2 feet (.6 metre) high.

Vinquoy Hill chambered cairn HY 560382 (metric map 5, 1-inch maps 5 & 6) On Eday island. Has a burial chamber 9 feet (2.7 metres) high.

Dwarfie Stane HY 244005 (metric maps 6 & 7, 1-inch maps 6 & 7) On the island of Hoy. This is the only rock-cut chambered tomb in Britain.

Blackhammer stalled cairn HY 414276 (metric maps 5 & 6, 1-inch maps 5 & 6) On Rousay island. Contains a burial chamber 42½ feet (12.3 metres) long.

Knowe of Yarso stalled cairn HY 403281 (metric maps 5 & 6, 1-inch maps 5 & 6) On Rousay island. Has a burial chamber 50 feet (15.2 metres) long by 25 feet (7.5 metres) wide.

Midhowe broch HY 371308 (metric map 6, 1-inch map 6) On Rousay island. A good example with substantial walls 15 feet (4.5 metres) thick. **Midhowe cairn,** an impressive stalled cairn 106

feet (32.6 metres) long and 42 feet (12.9 metres) wide, is close by.

Taversoe Tuick chambered cairn HY 426276 (metric maps 5 & 6, 1-inch maps 5 & 6) On Rousay island. An unusual two-storeyed tomb.

Quoyness chambered cairn HY 677378 (metric map 5, 1-inch map 5) On Sanday island. Six side chambers open off the main chamber.

Holm of Papa Westray chambered cairn HY 509518 (metric map 5, 1-inch map 5) On Holm of Papa Westray. A cairn with fourteen side chambers in its walls and rare carvings.

SHETLAND

Ness of Burgi Iron Age fort HU 388084 (metric map 4, 1-inch map 4) On the mainland, not far from Jarlshof. Stone ruins on a rocky promontory.

Broch of Mousa HU 457237 (metric map 4, 1-inch map 4) On Mousa island. The tower, the best preserved of its kind, is 40 feet (13.3 metres) high.

Stanydale 'Neolithic temple' and nearby standing stones HU 285503 (metric map 3, 1-inch map 2) On the mainland. The function of this structure is unknown.

Acknowledgements

Most of the photographs are from our own collection, but we wish to thank the following people and organisations for permission to use their copyright photographs. Our special thanks go to our indefatigable flying friend John Radford, who has spent so much of his valuable time enthusiastically securing some excellent aerial photographs for us.

The numbers refer to pages.

K. M. Andrew, 136, 145; Peter Baker Photography, 29; Barnaby's Picture Library, 15 (Bant's Carn); Bodleian Library, Oxford, 58 (top), 70; Brighton Museum and Art Gallery, 43 (right); British Tourist Authority, 166, 169 (bottom); Cambridge University Collection: copyright reserved, 37, 41 (top); J. Allan Cash, 163, 168, 173; Dorset County Museum, Dorchester, 34 (right); Crown copyright. Reproduced with permission of the Controller of Her Majesty's Stationery Office, 15 (Innisidgen and Porth Hellick Down), 63, 165, 167 (left), 170, 172, 174, 175; National Museum of Antiquities of Scotland, 167 (pottery and arrowheads); J. D. H. Radford, 34 (left), 35, 52, 55 (top), 56, 59, 62, 64, 78, 84, 86, 87, 91; Peter J. Reynolds, 42; Royal Albert Memorial Museum, Exeter, 28 (top); Crown copyright. Royal Commission on Ancient Monuments, Scotland, 157 (top); Scottish Tourist Board, 164; Edwin Smith, 103, 169 (top), 171; P. Thornton-Mallaby, 104 (both), 105; West Air Photography, Weston-super-Mare, 28 (bottom); Woodspring Museum, Weston-super-Mare, 72 (bottom); Geoffrey N. Wright, 157 (bottom).

Book List

GUIDEBOOKS

Peter Clayton, *Archaeological Sites of Britain*, Weidenfeld and Nicolson, 1976. Covers prehistoric and Roman sites in a continuous narrative.

'Discovering' books. These small paperback books, published by Shire Publications, now cover a wealth of subjects. Titles in the series 'Discovering Regional Archaeology' are: *The Cotswolds and the Upper Thames* by James Dyer, *North-Western England* by Barry M. Marsden, *North-Eastern England* by Barry M. Marsden, *Wales* by Ilid Anthony, *Wessex* by Leslie Grinsell and James Dyer, *Central England* by Barry M. Marsden, *South-Eastern England* by Edward Sammes, *South-Western England* by Leslie Grinsell, *Eastern England* by James Dyer. Also relevant are: *Discovering Archaeology in England and Wales* by James Dyer, and *Discovering Hill Figures* by Kate Bergamar.

James Dyer, *Southern England: An Archaeological Guide*, Faber, 1973 (hardback and paperback). An invaluable guide to the prehistoric and Roman remains of the area.

Richard Feachem, *A Guide to Prehistoric Scotland*, B.T. Batsford, 1963; 2nd edition 1977. A county-by-county guide to the most important visible remains.

Jacquetta Hawkes, *A Guide to the Prehistoric and Roman Monuments in England and Wales*, Cardinal/Sphere Books paperback, 1973. A highly readable tour of England and Wales.

Christopher Houlder, *Wales: An Archaeological Guide*, Faber, 1974. The prehistoric, Roman and early medieval field monuments described.

Phyllis Ireland, *Prehistoric Properties of the National Trust*, The National Trust, 1971. A small paperback guide with archaeological details of 34 sites in England and Wales.

Euan W. MacKie, *Scotland: An Archaeological Guide*, Faber, 1975 (hardback and paperback). An excellent guide, covering sites from earliest times to the 12th century AD.

Harold Priestley, *The Observer's Book of Ancient and Roman Britain*, Frederick Warne, 1976. A handy pocket guide giving basic archaeological information.

Regional Guides to Ancient Monuments: 1. Northern England, 2. Southern England, 3. East Anglia and the Midlands, 4. South Wales, 5. North Wales, 6. Scotland. H.M.S.O. These guides cover the sites which are in the care of the Department of the Environment, and so all periods, not just prehistoric, are included.

H.M.S.O. also publish various leaflets, guidebooks and archaeological reports for the Department of the Environment, and all are listed in Sectional List 27, 'Ancient Monuments and Historic Buildings', which also gives details on how to obtain them. The list can be obtained from Her Majesty's Stationery Office, Atlantic House, Holborn Viaduct, London EC1P 1BN.

Nicholas Thomas, *A Guide to Prehistoric England*, B.T. Batsford, 1960; 2nd edition, 1977. A county-by-county gazetteer of the major pre-Roman sites.

GENERAL BOOKS AND REGIONAL SURVEYS

J.R.L. Anderson and Fay Godwin, *The Oldest Road*: An Exploration of the Ridgeway, Wildwood House, 1975 (hardback and paperback). Both an evocative journey and practical guide.

Paul Ashbee, *Ancient Scilly*, David and Charles, 1974. Essential reading for visitors to the islands.

Keith Branigan, *Prehistoric Britain*, Spurbooks, 1976. An archaeological survey.

Peter Lancaster Brown, *Megaliths, Myths and Man*, Blandford Press, 1976. An introduction to astro-archaeology.

Aubrey Burl, *The Stone Circles of the British Isles*, Yale University Press, 1976. An archaeological survey, including their astronomical significance.

J. Forde-Johnston, *Prehistoric Britain and Ireland*, Dent, 1976. An archaeological survey of the surviving structures.

Aileen Fox, *South-West England 3500 BC – AD 600*, David and Charles, 1973. An area survey by an archaeologist.

Leslie Grinsell, *The Archaeology of Exmoor*, David and Charles, 1970. An area survey by an archaeologist.

Evan Hadingham, *Ancient Carvings in Britain*, Garnstone Press, 1974. Essential reading for anyone interested in cup and ring marks and other prehistoric carvings.

Evan Hadingham, *Circles and Standing Stones*, William Heinemann, 1975. A readable account of British prehistory, including a clear discussion of astronomical theories.

Gerald S. Hawkins, *Stonehenge Decoded*, Souvenir Press, 1966; Fontana paperback, 1970. A 'classic' study of Stonehenge's astronomical significance.

Gerald S. Hawkins, *Beyond Stonehenge*, Hutchinson, 1973. Further astronomical research and discovery.

A.H.A. Hogg, *Hill-Forts of Britain*, Hart-Davis, MacGibbon, 1975. A general account, with 160 sites described in detail.

Fred Hoyle, *On Stonehenge*, Heinemann Educational Books, 1977. An astronomer assesses the claims made for Stonehenge as an astronomical centre.

Lloyd Laing, *Orkney and Shetland: An Archaeological Guide*, David and Charles, 1974. Essential reading for visitors to the islands.

Lloyd Laing, *Ancient Scotland*, David and Charles, 1976. A guide to the remains, prehistory to the eighteenth century.

Euan W. MacKie, *Science and Society in Prehistoric Britain*, Elek Books, 1977. An examination of Thom's work and its implications. A new picture of our Neolithic ancestors emerges. A major work.

Euan W. MacKie, *The Megalith Builders*, Phaidon Press, 1977. An illustrated reassessment of Neolithic society.

Paul Pettit, *Prehistoric Dartmoor*, David and Charles, 1974. A readable survey of a rich archaeological area.

Regional Archaeologies series published by Heinemann Educational Books; titles so far published are: *Edinburgh and South-East Scotland, The Severn Basin, North Wales, South Wales, Yorkshire, South-West Scotland, The Roman Frontiers of Britain, Wessex, Ulster, East Anglia.*

Colin Renfrew, *Before Civilization*: The Radiocarbon Revolution and Prehistoric Europe, Jonathan Cape, 1973; Penguin paperback, 1976. An explanation of the implications of radiocarbon dating.

Colin Renfrew (editor), *British Prehistory*: A New Outline, Duckworth, 1974 (hardback and paperback). Six essays by leading prehistorians on the current picture of prehistoric Britain in the light of radiocarbon dating.

Peter J. Reynolds, *Farming in the Iron Age*, A Topic Book in the series Cambridge Introduction to the History of Mankind', Cambridge University Press, 1976. A fully illustrated and readable paperback, describing research into ancient farming.

A. Thom, *Megalithic Sites in Britain*, Oxford University Press, 1967, and *Megalithic Lunar Observatories*, Oxford University Press, 1971. Scholarly expositions of the astronomical theory.

Eric S. Wood, *Collin's Field Guide to Archaeology in Britain*, Collins, first published 1963, later revised. A useful and readable book, covering all kinds of visible traces left by man in Britain's countryside, from prehistoric to modern times.

Charles Woolf, *An Introduction to the Archaeology of Cornwall*, D. Bradford Barton, Truro, 1970. The rich archaeological history of one county described for the layman.

SOME THEORIES

Janet and Colin Bord, *Mysterious Britain*, Garnstone Press, 1972; Paladin paperback, 1974. An illustrated exploration of some of the stranger aspects of Britain's prehistory.

Janet and Colin Bord, *The Secret Country*, Elek Books, 1976; Paladin paperback, 1978. An interpretation of the folklore of ancient sites in the British Isles.

Michael Dames, *The Silbury Treasure*, Thames & Hudson, 1976. A new theory to explain this enigmatic mound.

Michael Dames, *The Avebury Cycle*, Thames & Hudson, 1977. A companion volume to *The Silbury Treasure*.

Francis Hitching, *Earth Magic*, Cassell, 1976. A readable enquiry into 'live' archaeology, considering leys and earth mysteries from opposing viewpoints.

John Ivimy, *The Sphinx and the Megaliths*, Turnstone Books, 1974; Abacus/Sphere Books paperback, 1976. An unusual theory linking British prehistoric sites with the Egyptian pyramids.

John Michell, *The View Over Atlantis*, Garnstone Press, 1969;
Abacus/Sphere Books paperback, 1973. The book which sparked off
the current interest in leys and earth mysteries.

John Michell, *The Old Stones of Land's End*, Garnstone Press, 1974. Some
leys of south-west Cornwall investigated, with an enquiry into the
mysteries of megalithic science.

John Michell, *A Little History of Astro-Archaeology*, Thames & Hudson,
1977. Describes the revolution in the academic view of prehistoric
society and its capabilities.

Paul Screeton, *Quicksilver Heritage*, Thorsons Publishers, 1974;
Abacus/Sphere Books paperback, 1977. A readable exploration of leys
and related theories.

Indexes

General Index
The references are to page numbers

Archaeology in Paladin Books

A Guide to Industrial Archaeology Sites in Britain   £4.95 ☐
Walter Minchinton
The 100 major sites featured in this book cover all aspects of industrial archaeology. Comprehensively illustrated with photographs and maps.

The Piltdown Men   £1.95 ☐
Ronald Millar
The case study of the most notorious hoax in the history of archaeology. Illustrated.

A Guide to the Hill-forts of Britain   £3.95 ☐
A H A Hogg
A fascinating reconstruction of Britain's past for those whose enjoyment of the countryside is enhanced by their understanding of its pre-Roman heritage. Illustrated.

Lucy: The Beginnings of Humankind   £2.95 ☐
Donald C Johanson & Maitland A Edey
Lucy is 3.4 million years old and is the oldest, most complete, best-preserved skeleton of any erect-walking human ancestor ever found. This single discovery has taught us more about early man than any other discovery so far. Illustrated.

The Cult of the Immortal   £2.95 ☐
Ange-Pierre Leca
A thorough and stimulating study of mummies and the ancient Egyptian way of death. Leca outlines the reasons why they were made and the deductions which modern science can draw from them; he describes the ancient methods of mummification, the various types and the associated rites. Illustrated.

The Mound People   £2.50 ☐
P V Glob
The successor to Professor Glob's widely acclaimed *The Bog People*, this engrossing study describes the Bronze Age aristocracy who were buried under specially constructed mounds and preserved by the action of tannic acid in the soil. Builds up a revealing picture of the daily life of our Bronze Age forebears. Illustrated.

To order direct from the publisher just tick the titles you want and fill in the order form.   PAL1182

Folklore in Paladin Books

A Dictionary of British Folk Customs   £2.95 ☐
Christina Hole
Every folk custom, both past and present, is described with its
history, development and present-day usage. The book includes a
nationwide calendar showing what happens, where and when.

The Classic Fairy Tales   £3.95 ☐
Iona and Peter Opie
Twenty-four of the best known stories in the English language are
presented in the exact words of the earliest surviving text or English
translation. Lavishly illustrated.

The Lore and Language of Schoolchildren   £2.95 ☐
Iona and Peter Opie
The classic study of the mysterious world and underworld of
schoolchildren – the games, the chants, the rites and the rituals
performed generation after generation by children all over Britain.

The People of the Sea   £1.95 ☐
David Thomson
The haunting record of a journey in search of the man-seal legends of
the Celts. 'Enthralling, spine-tingling, cliff-hanging' *Financial Times*

To order direct from the publisher just tick the titles you want
and fill in the order form.   PAL6082

History in Paladin Books

To order direct from the publisher just tick the titles you want and fill in the order form.   PAL7287

History in Paladin Books

The first two volumes in a new five-part series, **The Making of Britain** 1066–1939

The Norman Heritage 1066–1200   £3.95   ☐
Trevor Rowley
Through their energy and administrative ability, the Normans transformed the face of town and country alike. *The Norman Heritage* traces the impact of the Conquest on the British scene. Illustrated.

The Georgian Triumph 1700–1830   £3.95   ☐
Michael Reed
A vivid re-creation of the changes in the 18th century landscape caused by the adoption of new ideas and practices – from changes in architectural fashion to improvements in road-building. Illustrated.

To order direct from the publisher just tick the titles you want and fill in the order form.

PAL 7284

Anthropology in Paladin Books

Humankind   £2.95 ☐
Peter Farb
A history of the development of man. It provides a comprehensive
picture of how we evolved to reach our present state, and analyses
the remarkable diversity of human beings.

Shabono   £2.95 ☐
Florinda Donner
'A masterpiece . . . It is superb social science because in describing
her experiences among the Indians of the Venezuelan jungle Florinda
Donner plummets the reader into an unknown but very real world'
Carlos Casteneda

The Mountain People   £2.50 ☐
Colin Turnbull
A remarkable and gripping account of two separate periods in which
Turnbull lived with a declining African tribe, the Ik, in a mountain
area on the borders of Uganda and Kenya.

The Forest People   £2.50 ☐
Colin Turnbull
A fascinating study of the Pygmies of the Ituri Forest – a vast expanse
of dense, damp and inhospitable forest in the heart of Stanley's 'Dark
Continent'.

Lucy: The Beginnings of Humankind   £2.95 ☐
Donald C Johanson and Maitland A Edey
'A riveting book that is at once a carefully documented report, an
exciting adventure story, and a candid memoir of a brash young
palaeoanthropologist . . . What Lucy suggests about our forebears will
keep palaeoanthropologists arguing for years' ***Publishers Weekly***.
Illustrated

To order direct from the publisher just tick the titles you want
and fill in the order form.   **PAL2082**

History in Paladin Books

Africa in History   £2.95 ☐
Basil Davidson
Revised edition of 'one of the most durable and most literate guides to
contemporary knowledge of Africa' *Tribune*

A Higher Form of Killing   £2.50 ☐
Robert Harris and Jeremy Paxman
The escalating nuclear capabilities of the superpowers have been
extensively publicized. Less well documented has been the revival of
interest in chemical and biological weaponry. Drawing extensively
on international sources, this book chronicles for the first time the
secret history of chemical and germ warfare. Illustrated.

Decisive Battles of the Western World (Vols 1 & 2)   £3.95 ☐
J F C Fuller   each
The most original and influential military thinker Britain has ever
produced: his major work.

The Paladin History of England – the first three titles of the series are

The Formation of England   £2.95 ☐
H P R Finberg
This volume deals with Britain in the Dark Ages between Roman and
Norman conquests.

The Crisis of Imperialism   £3.95 ☐
Richard Shannon
England in the realm of Victoria. A time of development, expansion,
colonisation, enormous social upheavals and reform.

Peace, Print and Protestantism   £3.95 ☐
C S L Davies
C S L Davies' book deals with the period 1450–1558 encompassing
the reign of the Tudors and the breakaway from the Church of Rome.

To order direct from the publisher just tick the titles you want
and fill in the order form.   PAL7082

All these books are available at your local bookshop or newsagent, or can be ordered direct from the publisher.

To order direct from the publishers just tick the titles you want and fill in the form below.

Name _____

Address _____

Send to:
Paladin Cash Sales
PO Box 11, Falmouth, Cornwall TR10 9EN.

Please enclose remittance to the value of the cover price plus:

UK 60p for the first book, 25p for the second book plus 15p per copy for each additional book ordered to a maximum charge of £1.90.

BFPO 60p for the first book, 25p for the second book plus 15p per copy for the next 7 books, thereafter 9p per book.

Overseas including Eire £1.25 for the first book, 75p for second book and 28p for each additional book.

Paladin Books reserve the right to show new retail prices on covers, which may differ from those previously advertised in the text or elsewhere.